REFLECTIONS

— ON —

90
MINUTES IN HEAVEN

Powder Room Series Books

Reflections From the Powder Room on The Love Dare
Reflections on The Shack
Reflections on 90 Minutes in Heaven

Available from Destiny Image Publishers

REFLECTIONS
— ON —

90
MINUTES IN
HEAVEN

A TOPICAL DISCUSSION
BY WOMEN FROM
DIFFERENT WALKS OF LIFE

Writers: Shae Cooke, Tammy Fitzgerald, Donna Scuderi,
       Angela Rickabaugh Shears

Cover design and page layout: Dominique Abney

DESTINY IMAGE® PUBLISHERS, INC.

P.O. Box 310, Shippensburg, PA 17257-0310

"Speaking to the Purposes of God for This Generation and for the Generations to Come."

This book and all other Destiny Image, Revival Press, MercyPlace, Fresh Bread, Destiny Image Fiction, and Treasure House books are available at Christian bookstores and distributors worldwide.

For a U.S. bookstore near you, call 1-800-722-6774.

For more information on foreign distributors, call 717-532-3040.

Or reach us on the Internet: www.destinyimage.com.

ISBN 10: 0-7684-3131-X

ISBN 13: 978-07684-3131-5

For Worldwide Distribution, Printed in the U.S.A.

1 2 3 4 5 6 7 8 9 10 11 / 13 12 11 10 09

Contents

PREFACE

Here we are in The Powder Room again—bringing a whole new meaning to the "upstairs reading room." Now, instead of primping in front of fancy mirrors in a grand hotel in the city, we have returned to the comfortable surroundings of the powder rooms in our home sweet homes— slipped into our well-worn sweat pants (you know, the ones with the stretched-out elastic waistband) and the sweatshirt so soft and big that it hides the two bulges that have cruelly succumbed to gravity as well as all the other little pinch-an-inch love handles here and there.

My three powder puff sidekicks are with me again to share a refreshing flow of conversation, wit, and humor—real enough to touch today, spiritual enough to embrace tomorrow, and exciting enough to keep us reaching for our God-given destinies. Like you, we are traveling through life sometimes in control, sometimes not, sometimes joyfully, sometimes sorrowfully...and sometimes blindly. But traveling together makes the journey fun, and traveling with our heavenly Father always makes the journey a fabulous time of revelation and wonder.

Come sit awhile with us. The seats in front of our mirrors are comfortable...and the lights just bright enough to reveal things that may lead you toward fulfilling your destiny...or at least toward buying a new pair of sweats.

INTRODUCTION

With 3 million copies in print and as a *New York Times* and *USA Today* bestseller, *90 Minutes in Heaven* by Don Piper has made a difference in how many people view life—and Heaven.

As the third book in The Powder Room series, *Reflections on 90 Minutes in Heaven* exposes real-life-serious and not-so-serious discussion about life, death, and everything in between.

You will enjoy journeying along with us—four women whose beliefs, ideas, and experiences are as different as the lipstick we wear and the lives we lead. Realizing that discussions about the afterlife, eternity, immorality, and the hereafter have for centuries sparked intellectual deliberations, religious arguments, and personal introspection, we tackle these topics with all the finesse our stilettos, loafers, tennis shoes (and pink bunny slippers) will allow.

There is no doubt these wikipowderroom-type notes about *90 Minutes in Heaven* will create conversation in book clubs, classrooms, and kitchens as you question your views about life and death, as well as about Heaven and hell.

CHAPTER 1

HEAD-ON LIVING

Angela

When I started reading this book, I was prepared to read about a car accident, a guy who died, and what he saw in Heaven. Like 3 million other people who bought the book, I was hoping to get a glimpse of what Heaven is like. Before I opened the book I thought about how personal God is and that just reading about another's experience would not necessarily give me the truth about what *my* experience will be like when I meet Jesus. So with that in mind I began to read.

When an 18-wheeler meets a small car head-on, the consequence is usually fatal. Likewise, when we're going along in life and everything is hunkey dorey, we have a song in our hearts, but when an 18-wheeler comes straight at us, we better have more than a small metal frame protecting us. Health problems, financial issues, family concerns, coworker or boss confrontations, marriage issues, legal troubles, in-law intrusions—everyone faces a variety of head-on collisions throughout life. Without wearing the full armor of Christ, each of those collisions may be fatal. (See Ephesians 6:10-20.)

I've never been involved in a serious car crash, but I have been involved in numerous head-on collisions during which I have been broken and battered. Sometimes I forget to slip my arms into the breastplate of righteousness or my feet into the gospel of peace, and when that 18-wheeler is rumbling down the road toward me, I can't run as fast as I should to do the right thing. Sometimes I drop my shield of faith and my sword of the Spirit leaving me defenseless against a ruthless enemy. Through it all, though, the Lord comforts, guides, and heals me. Daily I try and remember to "dress for success"—the success God wants me to experience through His love and faithfulness.

Donna
◇◇◇◇◇◇◇◇◇◇

Oh, Angela! I can relate to the head-on living you describe! Life seems to come pre-loaded with bone-crushing moments. Take a few direct hits and you realize that bone-crushing doesn't necessarily mean life-ending. The sun really does come up tomorrow (that is, until it doesn't).

Getting over the impact doesn't mean we forget what being checked into the boards felt like (BTW, I'm watching a hockey game with one eye and blogging with the other). As resilient as humans are, we remember our head-on moments, and rightly so: we never look quite the same afterward and we want to be better prepared next time.

Whenever I see or hear about an accident, I mentally race through a checklist: I gasp. I pray. I imagine what the victims were doing...saying...thinking before impact. I wonder who is about to get a phone call telling them their loved one was involved in a wreck. I envision the victims' homes. The almost-empty coffee cup on the kitchen counter. The "to-do" list on the refrigerator.

You get the picture. So when I approached the first chapter, I (almost unconsciously) braced myself. I was about to hear the inside story of a deadly accident. I didn't know whether to cover my eyes or crane my neck. I did a little of both.

Don Piper answered my checklist questions. He confirmed the mundane aspects of the minutes prior to a crash, the thoughts preceding a moment of consequence: *Turn right or left? Take this road or that? Don't forget to pay the traffic ticket.*

He also reminded me how quickly everything can change— and how much we need God.

Shae

Mack truck moments...check my scars. Thank God for His new mercies around every bend, u-turn, or sudden stop.

Mercy, please God, if I see a sign for Prada shoes half-off and unexpectedly slam on the brakes or pull a U-ee. It is not my fault! Gluttony grasps the wheel, pops the gear into overdrive, and pushes the pedal to the metal. Jesus, take the wheel, please, especially when I'm supposed to be shopping for groceries.

Sometimes things are *beyond* my control. One minute I am at my prom, the next on the phone with my brother who tells me my mother perished in a fire. One minute I am wading waist deep in the calm sea, the next, a rogue wave knocks me over, sucks me under, and I am shark bait three miles offshore. Heaven-hell, Heaven-hell, life seems sometimes to foreshadow both.

I long for Heaven, sometimes for purely selfish reasons: as an escape and as a place that exists for my own benefit and pleasure, a place all about Shangri-la Happily-Ever-After-Shae. I know, I know, Heaven isn't about us at all, but in light of the daily grind, don't you just sometimes long for the wings of a dove as the psalmist did to fly away and be at rest? (See Psalm 55:6.)

I do hope Mr. Piper does Heaven justice. Anything less glorious than my spirit imagines will disappoint. Then again, what have we, as mortals, but words to describe the unseen, that which even the apostle Paul says, "...no mind can conceive." (See 1 Corinthians 1:9.) He also reminds us to *fix our eyes* on what is unseen because it is eternal, (see 2 Cor. 4:18) and C.S. Lewis noted, "If you read history you will find that the Christians who did the most for the present world were precisely those who thought most about the next one." Who would have thunk it?

Tammy

Way to make a girl feel nervous, y'all! Telling a 20-something about how life hits you head-on...scary! Even more so in light of this first chapter, where a man is just driving down the road of his life one day, suspecting nothing, and then *bam!* He steps into eternity. I think I'll be *walking* to the grocery store for *weeks*.

Of course, it's not like I've never experienced the surprising side of life before. I've been broadsided a couple times already, so I can relate a bit to what you're saying. Nice to know there's more where that came from, hehe. :P

At that same time, this can totally be encouraging. Like you said, Angela, God is there in the midst of disaster. When it comes to storms, He's the Captain to have at the helm. And even though this book starts off with perhaps the biggest disaster anyone could face—I can't think of anything much worse than sudden death—Piper is alive to tell about it. If God can carry him through death itself, surely He can bring me through *anything* to come. What's more, I hear that when He brings us through our storms, we often come out the other end stronger than before, with a powerful testimony of His faithfulness.

So...never mind. I'm not that scared after all. No matter how many times I get broadsided, to Him there are no surprises. He's got the map, the compass, the radar...all that jazz. Anchors aweigh! ^_^

Your Reflections

_____

_____

_____

_____

_____

_____

_____

_____

_____

_____

_____

_____

_____

_____

_____

_____

_____

_____

_____

_____

_____

_____

_____

_____

_____

_____

_____

_____

_____

_____

_____

CHAPTER 2

FOR HEAVEN'S SAKE

Angela

Who hasn't dreamt about Heaven? Well, I suppose atheists haven't, but I'd guess that most people daydream about their final exit. Me...I picture Jesus with His arms open wide and as I run to Him He scoops me up and swings me around in the clouds. Then hand in hand we walk through the pearly gates and down the streets of gold where on either side are gem-colored mansions with wide front porches where people are smiling as they rock on grand chairs and wave at us as they praise God the Father whose Being permeates the entire atmosphere. We stop in front of a beautiful house that reminds me of my childhood home—the door swings open and across the front porch and down the steps run my parents, grandparents, aunts and uncles all hugging and laughing and welcoming me. There is no talk of war, disease, terrorists, financial despair, political shenanigans, pirates, global warming, Octomom, Wall Street—just conversations about how much we love our Lord and Savior.

I was surprised that the author of *90 Minutes in Heaven* said that he didn't see Jesus. I always hoped that Jesus would be the first Person I would see upon entering Heaven. But I can only imagine in my pea-sized human brain that each person's homecoming will be unique—tailored special for each of us. Our God is so loving and faithful that I think He will provide us with an experience that will rock our senses and launch us into a world that we can't even begin to describe or imagine.

I look forward to meeting my Maker and worshiping Him forever more.

Donna
◇◇◇◇◇◇◇◇◇◇◇

Yes...imagine that! A world we can't begin to measure. What a far cry from the world in which we live. And what a welcome thought on this rainy...snowy...slippery...all-around creepy spring day when the news is packed with stories of mass murder, mayhem, and madness.

Not to mention politics.

Reset, Donna. Inhale. Imagine an atmosphere permeated with God's being. Ahhh...a place where every tear has been dried and every wound healed. Is it possible *not* to wonder about it at least once in your life? I suspect I'd have given it a thought even if atheism were my chosen path. Isn't that what faith is about? Those who have genuine faith that God does not exist must rise to the same challenge faced by those who are convinced that He does: in order to identify what you believe, you have to be very clear about what it is you are rejecting.

So, I believe there are places called *Heaven* and *hell*. Likewise, I have rejected the notion that a human being—specifically the human spirit—ceases to exist after death. The finality of death would be an easy enough concept to accept: You stop breathing. Your organs (including your brain) die. Your corpse rots. You are history.

Yet, I wonder which concept really is harder to wrap your mind around: the idea that we live forever (in one eternal place or another) or the belief that we are accidents of nature who live our lives utterly unconnected to anything or anyone bigger than us?

That is *the* rub, *the* decision each of us must make for ourselves. No. Don Piper's experience isn't mine...but I can almost imagine myself there in Heaven. In fact, I can practically feel it in my (very much alive) bones.

Tammy
◇◇◇◇◇◇◇◇◇◇◇

Angela, thanks for the reminder that God can make each of our homecomings unique—without it, my initial reaction to Chapter 2 was mostly disappointment. No Jesus? What could Piper mean, no Jesus? To me, that just didn't even sound like Heaven. In my mind, Heaven means *Jesus*—Jesus first, Jesus last, and Jesus all the way through, complete with God the Father and the Holy Spirit.

I've never needed or wanted a "heavenly welcoming committee" apart from Him. I figure I'll just start bumping into old friends and family while we're all dancing before the Lord. I'll take my reunion on the dance floor, thanks. ^_^

Needless to say, I'm relieved by the reminder that my homecoming could well be different from Piper's. Because, seriously, no Jesus? Don't even *go* there!

On the other hand, I nod in agreement with Piper when he says that words cannot describe the experience. I'm a big fan of words, but I'd like to think that when you get all the earthly hindrances stripped off your spirit and start to experience God without anything obscuring Him, human language is going to fall as woefully short as ever. A well-known hymn expresses this nicely:

> Could we with ink the ocean fill,
> And were the skies of parchment made,
> Were every stalk on earth a quill,
> And every man a scribe by trade,
> To write the love of God above
> Would drain the ocean dry;
> Nor could the scroll contain the whole,
> Tho stretched from sky to sky.
> (Frederick M. Lehman, "The Love of God,"
> 1917)

Did you know that these lines, which Lehman included in his hymn, were originally found scratched on a wall in an insane asylum? (See Frederick M. Lehman, "History of the Song, The Love of God," 1948.) Wow! Truly, the revelations of the Spirit of God are "meaningless nonsense" to those who don't know Him (see 1 Cor. 2:14 AMP).

Still, I'm looking forward to a Heaven where I can spend eternity using more than language to tell Jesus all about how awesome He is.

Shae

How profound, Tammy...more than language to tell Jesus how awesome He is....and right now, more than language to convey to the *world* how awesome He is without diminishing Him or reducing the awe factor. Imagine trying to describe to an unborn baby who has only known the shadows of his or her mother's womb what life on the outside is like. Try to describe to a person blind from birth, a person who has never seen a robin's egg, the ocean, the azure sky, or the color of a newborn's eyes, the color blue. Indeed, even God Himself is impossible to describe to a mere mortal. How do you describe a God who is brighter than a thousand suns, a God whose power makes an atomic warhead look like a firecracker, a God whose love is so *great*? Any attempt to describe Heaven I think also would be fruitless, except for the hope factor, the being with Jesus factor, and the euphoric relief that the one who experiences Heaven hasn't ended up in a pit of brimstone in the searing flames of hell. Juxtapose Piper's *90 Minutes in Heaven* with Bill Wiese's book *23 Minutes in Hell,* and you'll understand what I mean!

I applaud Mr. Piper for trying to describe Heaven, which is outside of any physical dimension, to those who have not been there; but it is quite different than I pictured in my spirit, and so far, less glorious than I imagined, because Jesus wasn't there. I understand my let down; Jesus *is* the joy and life of Heaven. Jesus is whom I want to see first. His absence in the visitation perplexes me. I am a mélange of emotions right now, but one thing for sure, the Life of Heaven, Jesus Christ, lives in me and is enthroned in my heart, and *that* quite simply, is indescribable *joy* . Heaven is where Jesus is, so I have heavenly experiences every day. What a thought— Heaven in our hearts...the ultimate love dimension!

Your Reflections

_____

_____

_____

_____

_____

_____

_____

_____

_____

_____

_____

_____

_____

_____

_____

_____

REFLECTIONS ON *90 Minutes in Heaven*

_____

_____

_____

_____

_____

_____

_____

_____

_____

_____

_____

_____

_____

_____

_____

CHAPTER 3

ANGELIC SURROUND SOUND

Donna

Music. Even from earth the right music can take me to heavenly places. How many times have a few short notes thrilled my heart or resurrected a sweet memory from long ago? Whether I'm absentmindedly browsing the produce aisle or consciously cranking my car radio (the volume of which goes to "11," by the way :) a searing guitar or inspired vocal can arrest me as surely as a S.W.A.T. team could. Music has this almost foolproof mechanism that taps into the deep places in my soul—a sublime, other-worldly location where thought, sight, sound, and emotion meld into a single sensation and elicit an unswerving response to the beauty that is sound.

It is, for me, a purely visceral "trigger." I suspect it is for most people. Of course, the wrong music can have an equally visceral, but far less desirable effect. Alas, that's an issue for another day. It's Don Piper's description of the music of Heaven that has arrested my soul for now and reminded me so pointedly that as good as life on earth is, Heaven remains the best of all destinations.

Often, in personal worship or during a corporate gathering, God captivates me through music. He draws me into His strong arms with melodies birthed, not in the heart of man, but by the breath of His Spirit. With a sound, He hoists me out of life's dissonant chambers, over the piles of debris, and past the inventory of damaged goods. Swoosh! Disappointment is dispelled in the effervescent rinse of His love.

Seamlessly, a song can transport me out of this material world and into the green pastures of fellowship with my Savior! In that meadow, I hear the hint of angel voices. It's marvelous. But it's nothing compared to what Don Piper heard.

Shae

Perhaps Donna, as believers on earth but spiritually seated with Christ in the heavenlies, we are more in tune with the music of Heaven than we realize! There have been increased claims of angelic voices and music in worship services, sparking a blaze of interest in the subjects of God, angels, and Heaven. In many cases, people see colors, as Mr. Piper described he did in his heavenly visitation, and often moving and merging in harmony with the sounds.

In the winter of 1981, I heard what had to be an angelic choir as I passed below the open windows of a home situated on a dusty back street in a village on the Baja of Mexico. At first I heard the sounds in the distance, but like the shining star that led the shepherds to the Christ Child, the music "magnetically" drew me to that place of beautiful melodic worship. While it was apparent that people were in that small upper room and singing, something not of this world accompanied their worship. The harmony was a supernatural wonder, sounding like a thousand blended voices, sometimes gentle and sweeping like a symphony of endless hazy rolling hills, and in parts, rising and falling like an orchestral ocean tide, in a perfect blending of chords and notes unfamiliar to my ears. Suddenly, under deep conviction for having backslid from the Lord for a few years, and feeling a weighty beautiful presence around me, I rededicated and yielded my life back to God, and oddly, felt a strong longing for my heavenly home and the arms of Jesus.

I often think about how the Bible says that the angels get excited when the lost come to the Lord. Surely, therefore, these beautiful creatures must yearn to mingle their voices and music with ours to pour out praises to the One whom they and we so desperately and deeply adore. Keep your ears open, girls!

Angela

Years ago I watched *Touched by an Angel* on TV and I liked thinking that the angel of death was this really nice guy who accompanied the dying to Heaven. Before that show I really never thought believers needed to be ushered into Heaven, but maybe we do. After all, angels do help us through uncharted territories; for example an angel was with young unmarried Mary when she learned that she would be our Savior's mother, angels were with the shepherds, Joseph heard from an angel about imminent danger, and angels ministered to saints in both the Old and New Testaments—and most of us have been protected by angels unaware.

Then there was the movie *City of Angels* that I happened to click into one wintry stay-at-home Sunday afternoon. I immediately texted one of my movie-guru daughters and asked if it had a happy ending (the only kind of anything I watch). "Yes, I think so," was her reply. Great, because I really like Meg Ryan. Watch, watch, watch, um...cry at the end. What!? Text: "She died!" Text: "Oh, sorry, I must have been thinking of another movie."

Dying is sad stuff for those left behind feeling the loss of "one less egg to fry." But reading the author's experience softens the separation because we can imagine loved ones in a place where the "holy swoosh of wings" and beautiful songs are eternally sung by choruses whose only motivation is to worship and praise God almighty. No commercials, no commentary, no underlying themes like "Paul is dead" played backward. In this life I really enjoy traditional gospel music and contemporary Christian music (an original Jesus Freak fan). In the next life, I'm looking forward to constant sweet angelic surround sound. (I'm just keeping my fingers crossed that they aren't into country or bluegrass up there.)

Tammy

It really is something to think of music perfected—to try to imagine what the soul-songs of all humanity down through the ages will sound like when they reach the place where every broken note is healed. And every song will be only praise and wonder and adoration of the only One who was ever worth singing about—the God who was in every small beauty we ever admired in life, making it something to sing about. He's been the subject of our joy through every century, and only in Heaven will all that ecstatic music finally break free and find perfect, crystalline focus on Him.

Wow, what a song that will be! And Angela, I think even country music will find a perfect form there, becoming delightful to Him and to all who hear it. ^_^

Still, the fact that Piper didn't see God kinda bums me out. I mean, was He hiding Himself from Piper? (I hope He wouldn't hide Himself from me!) I can sort of understand Piper's explanation, but I question it too. Seeing God would have made him not want to return to earth? It doesn't really seem like he wanted to anyway. He was just gone, back on earth. No choice offered, as far as we know.

If he was going to return anyway, why couldn't he at least get a glimpse of God first? Just a little bit? A chance to say "Hi! You're amazing!" Maybe get a quick hug...OK, perhaps I'm just daydreaming for myself here. ^_^

My point is simply that I can't imagine going to Heaven and not seeing Jesus. I feel that all the joy and light and even the perfection of celestial music would be a bit anticlimactic if I didn't get to see His face.

Your Reflections

_____

_____

_____

_____

_____

_____

_____

_____

_____

_____

_____

_____

_____

_____

_____

_____

_____

_____

_____

_____

_____

_____

_____

_____

_____

_____

_____

_____

_____

_____

_____

CHAPTER 4

PRAY FOR ME

Donna

A t a Christian educators' conference a dozen or so years ago, I took a flying leap in the hotel atrium where breakfast was being served. I use the word *flying* circumspectly; a man who sat reading his newspaper as I sailed by later told me that two legs attached to an airborne body cruised by him at eye level and a frightening rate of speed. (The legs, and body for that matter, were mine—a scary shade of white capped off by even whiter pumps.)

The flight wasn't pretty. The landing was pitiful. Unable to get up, I remained splayed on the floor in the midst of a hundred or more Christians who seemed to freeze mid-gasp. (Did I mention that I was wearing a dress?) Finally, a gentleman wearing a name badge from the Christian educators' conference approached me much the way a zoo visitor would approach an unsecured lions' den. He asked timidly, "How can I help you?"

Embarrassed though I was, getting up wasn't my first priority; prayer was. Tilting my head in disbelief the way a dog gawks at a new bowl, I asked, "Would you please pray with me?" Surrounded by a company of Bible-believing Christians, I had to ask somebody to pray! Needless to say, I and the co-worker with whom I was traveling have enjoyed many belly laughs over that piece of irony.

On a *much* more serious note, Don Piper's story reminds us how profound the business of prayer can be. Because Dick Onerecker seized the moment and *prayed for a dead man* (despite his doctrinal beliefs), Don Piper is alive to tell the world about his first trip to Heaven! Only God knows all the implications of Dick's simple act of faith.

Shae

I can one-up ya! I recall walking out of a swank hotel powder room and into a crowded lobby to wait for a colleague, with my skirt tucked into my pantyhose *and* trailing a long stream of soggy toilet paper. I only discovered what I had done an hour later when I had to powder my nose again. Can you believe, no one told me? I just thought all the pointing, oh my goshes, and stares were because I looked hot—lol. Dying of embarrassment, I stayed in the bathroom until I was sure the crowd of tourists waiting for their buses had departed. I've been in therapy ever since! Oh, I needed prayer right then and there, for sure!

Several years ago, I witnessed a car run down a bicyclist on a busy main road in downtown Vancouver. Grabbing my first aid kit, I ran to the victim who lay unconscious and bleeding, appealing to the onlookers to call 911 while I checked her vitals. (I recommend everyone take an emergency first-aid course and keep a stocked kit in the car, there is nothing worse than feeling helpless in a life and death situation). I'd done all that I could do to physically help this young woman, so since I was already kneeling, lifted my arms, and appealed to the Lord to save her, shedding inhibition, not caring who saw, or what anyone thought, though sensing growing curiosity. By and by, the ambulance came and the team took over. After I had spoken to the police, a posse approached me. "Were you praying...were you actually praying for her?" I nodded yes, a little embarrassed, not quite remembering the details in the adrenaline of the moment. "I have never, ever seen anyone openly pray for an accident victim before," one said. *That* was a shock. Before long, we all engaged in a discussion about the Lord. I don't know if the woman lived, but I do believe my prayers "availethed" much!

Angela

After years of editing and writing for a Christian publishing company and other assorted Christian and secular groups, organizations, and businesses, I've read almost everything (well, that's probably a stretch) that has been written about prayer. From Augustine to Spurgeon to T.D. Jakes to a myriad of dissections of the Lord's Prayer, most Christians have an opinion about how, when, why, and the what-for of prayer. Not one to keep my opinions to myself, I must say that prayer to me (for the past almost 30 years since coming to know Jesus as my personal Savior) is a continuing conversation with an almighty God. If I'm not thanking Him for Jesus, our family's good health, the warm sunshine, food on the table, gas in the car, my nice soft pillow, and various other big and little blessings, I'm talking to Him about world events (as I am refreshing the Drudge Report about every 30 minutes), or I'm wondering with Him about how I can become the person He wants me to be.

I believe Scriptures that tell us to (paraphrasing) "ask and you will receive," "where two or more are gathered in His name, He is in the midst," "pray in your closet and the Father will reward you openly," "the prayer of faith shall save the sick," and all the many references to prayer in the Bible. Communicating with God is as vital to life as the air we breathe.

There is a prayer "e-chain" at our church and the pastor sends out e-mails to the pray-ers when a request comes to his attention. Much improved from the phone chain of years past when there was inevitably dog, kids, television, vacuuming, and/or cooking noise competing with a serious discussion, now I can concentrate on the need and pray more single-mindedly. With so many issues confronting and confounding us today, I remember Mother Teresa's quote, "If you can't feed 100 people, then feed just one." I have a similar outlook—one prayer at a time.

Tammy

Prayer. It's everything from long conversations with God, public and private, to quick words of gratitude thrown heavenward with a smile, to the deep, anguished soul-cries of the lost and the persecuted. Our spirits are born into life with a prayer. The shortest prayer I ever prayed—"Lord, I surrender"—brought about the most profound change of my life.

Isn't it strange how so many people believe that prayer can bring a dead spirit to life, yet reject the idea that it can do the same for a dead body? It's kind of like saying, "Oh, the spirit is simple enough for prayer to save it. They're both abstract, intangible things, so they go together. The body is another matter though. The body is just too complicated, too solid and real to be fixed by something like prayer." (OK, so maybe most people wouldn't actually *say* this, but it's true that this kind of thinking is out there.)

How wrong this idea is! Prayer—weak and ineffective? We need to see that notion *changed*. The Church needs to realize the true power of their prayers to rock the world and bring even the dead back to life. Just ask Don Piper—no really, ask him! He's alive to tell us all about it because people prayed, starting right here in a smashed car.

What's more, where did we get the idea that the physical world is harder to affect with prayer than the spiritual? God is absolutely in control of both, and we know that "this world in its present form is passing away" (1 Cor. 7:31). Let's not be cowed by brokenness we can see and touch. Let's go after healing for *everything*—physical and spiritual—knowing that our perfect, loving, infinitely *good* God is listening and loves to answer our prayers!

Your Reflections

_____

_____

_____

_____

_____

_____

_____

_____

_____

_____

_____

_____

_____

_____

_____

_____

_____

_____

_____

_____

_____

_____

_____

_____

_____

_____

_____

_____

_____

_____

_____

CHAPTER 5

DEAD MAN SINGING

Donna

The impossible is possible. The irrevocable can be re-voked. A death sentence can become a new lease on life. And all of it can happen because God really is *God*.

All of the above statements are true. I believe them with every fiber of my being. And if I didn't believe any of them, I would still have to reckon with the inconvenient matter of a dead man singing. Who could explain that away? *A dead man singing!*

There's a perfect example of a spiritual light show not meant to be kept under a bushel. No. This irrepressible ray of hope is suitable for the very tallest of lampstands (see Matt. 5:15) and any other forms of celebration that come to mind. Just thinking about it makes me want to jump up and down, do cartwheels, sing the national anthem, and strum "Amazing Grace"—all at the same time!

Then, after I catch my breath (oxygen, anyone?) I'll run (more oxygen, please) and tell the story to friends and family members who are struggling. One at a time, I'll put my arms around them and remind them (and myself) in gloriously improper English that even when it's over, it ain't over. Then the two of us can do cartwheels together, harmonize on the national anthem, and play dueling guitars to "Amazing Grace"—all at the same time.

It's easy to imagine Dick Onerecker's ebullience as he ran to tell the EMT that the dead man was singing. Dick's simple act of obedience proved to be a ticket to the supernatural—a front-row seat in the arena of the miraculous. The man whose body lay in floppy shreds in a hopelessly wrecked automobile was *singing*!

And he escaped the threat of brain injuries. How miraculous!

Angela

Reading how the praying pastor pleaded with EMTs to believe him when he said that the dead man in the demolished car was actually alive threw my mind into the Books of John and Luke where Mary Magdalene pleaded with Jesus' disciples to believe her—she saw an empty tomb, she saw two angels in white, and her Master spoke to her. (See John 20:18-31 and Luke 24:10-12.) Speaking of Mary and the women who had gone to the tomb with spices and ointments, the disciples and the others thought "their words seemed to them as idle tales, and they believed them not (Luke 24:22 KJV). Only after Peter went to the sepulchre and saw the empty tomb and the "linen clothes laid by themselves" did he wonder if the women were right. Only after Thomas saw the nail holes in Jesus' hands and His pierced side did he believe Jesus was alive.

How do we handle situations when people don't believe us? Don't believe that Jesus is the Son of God? Don't believe that He died and rose again to redeem all of humanity?

It's hard. It's hard to realize a member of your family may not have known Christ before he or she died. It's hard to know that millions around the globe have never heard about the Father's saving grace. It's hard to face our reluctance to spread the Good Word more often. Jesus wept when He looked out over Jerusalem. We weep when we read news that is filled with child abuse, corrupt politicians, murders, and the evil that pervades the earth.

What can we do? We can believe, and we can sing His praises loud and clear.

"Blessed are they who have not seen, and yet have believed" (John 20:29).

Shae

Tra la la! I have found that heavenly things possess a greater reality than do earthly ones. Reality to the paramedics was that Piper was dead and *not* coming back. "The man in the red car is deceased...body mangled...it has been 90 minutes..." In other words, "Dead is dead dude. Lips are white, skin is chalky, and the body is 90 minutes away from rigor mortis. I checked him myself...no vitals...pray if you want but it'll be like expecting a rock to rise and walk outta here." Hope finite.

The Baptist preacher insisted he had to pray for the stranger, whom he could plainly see was lifeless. By all appearances, Piper was a goner; probably minutes away from sporting a toe tag. Onerecker climbed out of his own finite comfort zone, touched the bloody corpse, and using prayer, faith, and worshipful song, created a new reality, a present and real heavenly reality according to the promise of Jesus. "Therefore, I say unto you, all things whatsoever ye pray and ask for, believe that ye received them, and ye shall have them...that your joy may be full." Hope infinite.

How often I pray in the problem, without thinking, by telling God how big the mountain is. It is like telling God, "It's impossible but...." Imagine if the preacher had prayed, "Oh God, this man is so shredded, he is in pieces, as dead as a doornail. Do what You can." Instead, he pulled on Heaven calling forth something that was not, praying and believing for things he couldn't see. The realm of possibility broke through bringing the true Jaws of Life to Piper and I would hope to think, the reality of miracles to the doubtful and skeptical paramedic. I wonder what would happen in more cases if emergency teams prayed over their accident victims; more dead men walking and singing, to be sure!

Tammy

Right at the end of this chapter, Dick Onerecker said, "I wish I could pray like that all the time." I'm sure many of us at one time or another feel that "holy jealousy." We yearn to see God's awesome supernatural power at work and to see the miraculous with our own eyes. So many sigh and say, "If only I could have the experience, the confidence, the courage to pray like *that* all the time."

Body of Christ—*you can!* You *can* have that assurance, you *can* see His irrefutable miracles at work in the world, you *can* pray and know that your God hears and is right there, ready to back you up. Just take two steps. Dick Onerecker did; here's what they were.

First, he heard and heeded the voice of God. He recognized the sound of God giving him a heavenly directive. We as Christians need to grow gigantic spiritual Dumbo ears. We need to be able to hear what God is saying to us in every moment, developing our sensitivity to His still, small voice through practice, practice, practice so that we don't miss the gift of His direction.

Second, he stepped out and took a risk. He obeyed God's order even though he risked looking foolish in front of other people. When the rubber met the road, he decided that God's voice ranked higher than the voice of the world, and he followed that leading.

That's all we need to do. Hear him and obey Him, even when it's risky. He'll show up on our side; He's the one giving the orders in the first place, after all! He's not going to leave us hanging. And, if believers will follow, He'll lead us to pray prayers that are incredible and see answers that are impossible for anyone but Him.

Your Reflections

_____

_____

_____

_____

_____

_____

_____

_____

_____

_____

_____

_____

_____

_____

_____

_____

CHAPTER 6

DEAD OR ALIVE

Angela

Thankfully I've only been a hospital patient three times in my life—twice to deliver beautiful daughters, and another time to have all the baby-making parts removed. All three times ended with wonderful results. But I hope and pray that I never see the inside of a hospital again. I know and have heard of way too many people who have gone in for "routine" procedures and were either permanently disabled or died.

Reading all that the author went through—the pain, the decision made for him, his mutilated body, the uncertainty of a healthy future—made me shiver. I can understand why he asked, "God, is this what I came back for? You brought me back to earth for this?" There's a saying that if men were the ones to have children, the human race would die out in short order; and I do admit that most men I know have a low tolerance for pain. But this man's body went through major trauma.

In 2007, Dr. Kevorkian—Dr. Death—was released after serving eight years in prison for being convicted of injecting lethal drugs into a 52-year-old man with Lou Gehrig's disease. He claimed that he assisted 130 people commit suicide. His premise: people have the right to decide if they want to continue living with chronic or terminal illnesses or to die. Many said he was "playing God" when he built his "suicide machine" that allowed the person to administer lethal doses of drugs.

In the midst of pain, the author struggled with wanting to return to Heaven. Rather, his wife sought out a good friend who launched a prayer vigil that lightened his suffering.

How many people right now could be given hope if they knew the power of prayer? Prayer on behalf of others (intercession) is a blessing for all involved. Bless and be blessed today.

Donna
◇◇◇◇◇◇◇◇◇◇◇

Hats off to the David Gentiles of this world. While it's easy enough to say, "I will pray for you," saying "We won't let you die," is another matter. David Gentiles made a solemn commitment to carry his fallen brother across the next mile marker in his marathon recovery.

David Gentiles and the other prayer warriors were determined. When Don Piper was "out of gas," they promised to put their faith on the line and pray him through. When you're physically and emotionally stretched as far as Don Piper was (no pun intended), having someone offer to pick up the baton and run for you means *everything*. It's an act of grace that allows those who are crushed to breathe again. I saw that kind of grace many years ago when my mother was critically ill and unable to eat. If she were to have any chance at all, she would need nutritional support. We took her to see the late Dr. Robert Atkins, who had helped me to recover from devastating immune issues a year or two earlier.

Dr. Atkins was forthright with my dad, my brother, and me. He concurred with the oncologists that my mother's chances of survival were extremely low; but he was willing to do whatever he could to help her nutritionally. My mother was worried about all the special arrangements he would have to make to accommodate her; she was also beating herself up for her condition (she'd been a smoker). Dr. Atkins took her hands in his and said, "Lillian, you needn't heap blame on yourself and you needn't worry about the details. Let us do the worrying."

My mother's despairing countenance brightened at this demonstration of grace...and the love that was behind it. Dr. Atkins had a heart like David Gentiles.

Shae

This chapter reads like the Book of Job in its explicit details of Don Piper's injuries and suffering. As Job's love for the Lord remained strong, so, it appears, does Don's love. He had some complaining and questioning moments—the suffering was intense, but thus far, he refuses to shake his fist at God, and persists in trusting Him even in the hand dealt to him. When he did falter, God rallied the troops to intercede on his behalf. Perhaps Don's positive outlook was the result of his first-hand experience of Heaven, which for most of us is a future hope we can only imagine, where there will be no more tears or pain. He ultimately knew that his suffering would not be forever, having seen his loved ones and friends who had gone on before, *intact.*

Since you mentioned childbirth, Angela, I liken this type of endurance and hope to that of a mother having her second child. She knows that the pain disappears once the baby is born, (some mom's might refute that!). When I was in difficult back labor with my son, *sans* any mode of medical pain relief, (not my choice...*p-a-leeeease...give me the gas)...*I recall one point freaking out because I lost sight of the promised outcome. Had I been able to conceive and have another child, I think my pain threshold and endurance would have remarkably improved. Ditto for a man experiencing the process!

Someone once said that suffering makes a person either bitter or better. Did I mention my bitter moment? I damned my son's father to hell and screamed, "You will never ever touch me again, you brute!" Ouch! Trust that my bitterness was short-lived and human because I knew God's character, having trusted Him in other things. I am wondering, is *this* how Mr. Piper endured his living hell? I think, yep, and as such, he could determine God trustworthy and true when his body fell apart.

Tammy

With orderlies taking out the remains of those who didn't make it, it's pretty clear that Don Piper was in "the valley of the shadow of death"—death surrounded him on all sides in the ICU. He was among the dying, and he was there as one near death himself. Unable to do anything for himself, he experienced having his human impulse for independence thwarted, replaced instead by forced dependence.

David Gentiles and an army of prayer warriors cried out to Heaven through a night that would have otherwise claimed Piper's life. Doctors and nurses took the ruins of his body and began to patch them back together. And Eva, his wife, made a decision for both of them, stepping out in faith and believing that the Ilizarov frame could save her husband's leg. All these people stepped into the valley of death with Piper, rallying with him and struggling to bring him through.

Of course, God was there too, answering Piper's prayers and remaining with him. He keeps His promise—He is always with us. At the same time, however, He sometimes also brings us comfort and support in the form of other people, as He did for Piper.

It's a blessing with a lesson attached—learning to let go of the reins and trust others with the control you can no longer handle is an uphill battle against all our fleshly inclinations. Yet it's a priceless lesson. The person who has learned to surrender, trusting God and others, has picked up one of the best Kingdom skills out there!

Your Reflections

_____

_____

_____

_____

_____

_____

_____

_____

_____

_____

_____

_____

_____

_____

_____

_____

_____

_____

_____

_____

_____

_____

_____

_____

_____

_____

_____

_____

_____

_____

_____

_____

_____

CHAPTER 7

A GOOD DOSE OF FAITH

Angela

How many times have you heard someone tell you all the gory details of their surgery and/or illness? TMI! And how many times have you wished and hoped that they would stop before getting too graphic? Can you top this one? I was sitting in the chair at the beauty salon getting my hair trimmed when in walked an acquaintance. She proceeded to tell us all about her bout with breast cancer and we all were attentive and concerned. Then all of a sudden she started to pull up her blouse to show us what her mastectomy incision looked like and I thought I was going to lose my lunch at just the thought, so before anything was revealed I made a polite but hasty exit.

I'm a compassionate but not very medically inclined person. My family always dug out their own splinters and cleaned up their own messes—in fact we all have an aversion to throwing up. I can count on one hand how many times any of us have done that in the past 10+ years. Fortunately we are from "healthy stock" and have had very few illnesses. But wow, are we the exceptions it seems, judging from all the drug ads and "medical moments"!

Along with all the drugs that most doctors prescribe for anything at anytime for anyone, our nation seems to be so self-focused on how high our blood pressure, sugar, or cholesterol is that we don't take the time to seek God's will in every area of our lives. Rather, most seek a doctor's advice and take his or her word as gospel. Gee, that might sound harsh, but I know too many people who are taking too many drugs when all they need is a healthy diet, exercise, and a good dose of consulting the Great Physician.

Donna

Health is a precious commodity and life is more fragile than we realize. Don Piper talks about never again taking "simple physical ability for granted." The morning of his accident, he probably showered, shaved, brushed his teeth, and combed his hair like every other guy at the conference. Little did he know that, by noon, those simple acts would become physical impossibilities.

The thought of his physical loss is staggering. It leaves us to wrestle with the idea that life *really can* change in an instant. Intellectually, I understand that; but since I've never experienced such incapacitation, I surely have no clue as to what it actually means.

Some injured veterans know all too well; so do many crime victims and, of course, other accident victims. I think of Christopher Reeve because he's someone we all "knew" before and after. We saw him in full physical bloom, then peered from afar into his radically transformed life. How could a series of mundane circumstances coalesce into such a horribly complicated outcome?

No wonder Don Piper had initial doubts about whether his survival was a blessing or a curse. How he wanted to have his life put back the way it had been before the accident! I'm guessing he knew deep down that the world as he knew it was gone forever. But there it was..."new normal"...a paradigm by definition unattractive, not only because it was thrust upon him, but also because it cost him and his loved ones so dearly.

Because of Piper's book, we know that God's plan of blessing was already in motion; but when Piper was flat on his back, incapacitated and in agonizing pain, blessing surely seemed far, far away.

Shae

Good gravy, Marie. I agree, sometimes our blessings seem far away, but thank goodness, Mr. Piper does not cop a survivalist attitude. This is deadly in suffering for a host of reasons—

and I am preaching to the choir here. The survivor mind-set has never released faith for what I need, and I discovered much later, that it overshadowed and diminished God in the eyes of the world. I am guilty of being content with less than God has for me; with being grateful for just slipping through, barely making it, or just breaking even in this life. I have shortchanged others and myself in my expectations. And I have shortchanged God in not giving Him those opportunities to radically transform things in my life and within my sphere of influence.

I have a relative who hung on by a thread through her cancer treatments, becoming more embittered every day. Well-meaning people would encourage her to "Hang in there, hold on," but to what? The thread? No wonder she was bitter, constantly dangling off a cliff like that, never knowing when her life would go "poof"! How much better to be held by the strong arm of God who clasps us with His promises, making us prisoners of hope, and giving Him opportunity to dazzle the world with His love and power.

I say it is time we tossed out the "I survived" stickers for the "God put me back together again" testimonies; something *90 Minutes in Heaven* does very well. Thus far, this is what sets it apart from the average tragedy to triumph story, feeding my faith to move from problem to promise, from impossibility to possibility with God.

Tammy

Angela, I'm with you on the TMI aspect of part of this book

already! What's more, I always considered myself to have a pretty tough stomach. Not that I'm bragging about being desensitized, but facts are facts—it's hard to bother me with gore, yet parts of this medical stuff sure freak me out! Yikes!

Praise the Lord for giving some people strength greater than mine in the area of medicine! He did an amazing thing by gifting certain individuals with the strength and the skills to be doctors and nurses. What would we do without them? Certainly Don Piper wouldn't be alive if not for their dedication and tenacity and patient care.

Dr. Houchins is the kind of doctor I'd want—refusing to give up on me, even if I have. Scratch that, he's the kind of *friend* I want in my life. People who are willing to do anything to push you when you need to be pushed are sometimes too rare and precious. Of course, people like David Gentiles are priceless too—sometimes we just need others there whom we can rely upon and trust in. But sometimes we also need a swift kick in the pants...at least, I do!

I've got my eye out for a Dr. Houchins-type friend. In the meantime, I'm happy to report that the Holy Spirit isn't always a "still, small voice"—when He needs to be, He can be quite blunt with His thick-headed daughter!

Your Reflections

_____

_____

_____

_____

_____

_____

_____

_____

_____

_____

_____

_____

_____

_____

_____

_____

_____

_____

_____

_____

_____

_____

_____

_____

_____

_____

_____

_____

_____

_____

_____

_____

_____

_____

CHAPTER 8

I WANT TO GO BACK

Angela

Dear fellow bloggers, I must give you all credit for writing such interesting and penetrating thoughts about this book. You are very nice and polite and good at looking beyond and between the page after page of depressing prose. I was hoping that it might take a turn for the better, but Chapter 8 starts off with how the people who visit him make his "situation worse." Huh? And my heart broke thinking about how his wife may have felt knowing he was despondent because of the pain he was going through as a result of the very hard decision she had to make about his leg—experimental bone growth device or amputation.

Many times he wonders why he was "brought back from a

perfect Heaven to live a pain-filled life on earth. No matter how hard I tried, I couldn't enjoy living again; I wanted to go back to Heaven." In my mind, that is not our decision to make...or even question. God knows the best time for each of us to leave this life and move into the next. God's timing is perfect. God is in control. Reading that he wanted to be "free from my miserable existence and die" is hard for me to understand. I kept thinking about his loving family, his young children, his concerned parents, his caring congregation.

It seems the physical body is much easier to heal than the mind. His depression affected all those who loved him. Not presuming for a second to know God's thoughts, I respectfully guess that his heavenly Father didn't want him to use his experience in Heaven to keep him from living and loving on earth.

Shae

I wonder—will we wear shoes in Heaven...and, if the devil wears Prada...oh my gosh...*no* Prada...lol. Perhaps white almond bark chocolate, Jamaican Blue Mountain coffee...? I think it pleases God that we yearn and pine for Heaven. Is it so wrong that we want to escape this sinful, painful world? Does it mean we are depressed if we do? Even if Don were not lying there as broken in body as Humpty Dumpty, I suspect he would be longing to return to Heaven, without disrespect to his wife, family, and friends. The king's horses and men *were* having trouble putting him back together again.

Like a dangling carrot (karat!), God gives us just enough glimpses in the Bible of Heaven to *compel* our curiosity and constant reaching for that place the Bible calls "a heavenly country," a place with gates made of single pearls (thoughts of monster oysters aside). I mean, just the lure of precious jewels, streets paved with gold, mansions, and crowns, is enough to make any girl crazy for Heaven; the greatest draw though, meeting Him. So I cry out in a soulful Yiddish type of way, "God, take me away, take me home," when things get tough. Does that mean I need to be on Prozac, or that this is sin or weakness? We *are* pilgrims on a journey there—some of us just want to get there quicker. Don has more arrows in his back than most pilgrims have. I understand where he is at, and I am confident God understands.

It is ironic that the 12 gates in Heaven are made of pearls, because pearls do speak of beauty out of pain. The oyster goes through a painful irritating process to form the pearl. I hope when I am lying on my deathbed or in a life/death situation that no one tries to dissuade or discourage me from wanting to go "home," because I think it would actually kill my resolve to get better. This longing for Heaven...I think it is a part of our spiritual DNA, and it is what does give us hope to endure our present realities.

Donna
◇◇◇◇◇◇◇◇◇◇◇

A beloved former pastor of mine often says that "in our better moments" we easily believe everything God promises. To me, this dear man's words capture the dynamics of faith. In his better moments, Abraham believed God's promise of a son. In his better moments, David danced with abandon in worship of his God. Yet, both men experienced moments of anguish in which they were rendered transparent before the Almighty. In their transparency, despair was laid bare and mercy applied.

God's Word says that Jesus is touched with the feeling of our infirmities (see Heb. 4:15). Moments of weakness come— even days when His promises seem so ethereal as to waft aimlessly into the ozone. Don Piper lived through hard places. Endless days of unbearable pain and excruciating uncertainty rendered him transparent to God and others. No longer could he present only his strong side. He *was* strong in faith. He *was* walking with God. Yet, when his life was divinely preserved (isn't that everyone's prayer?) he begged God to release him from his miracle. Ironic, yet real.

Was he trying to make a decision that is only God's to make? I honestly don't think so. My guess is that he was tried by agony to the very brink of breaking. I can picture him in a dark night of suffering as he whispered, "Daddy, I don't think I can handle this. Can't I just come home with You?"

In the midst of doubt and fear, when the lifeline seemed ready to snap, God carried Don Piper, not because Piper was strong and gave Him all the right answers, but because the Father loves him. God escorted Piper, broken body and soul, into *more* life and *greater* faith...even when he wasn't sure he wanted to go.

Tammy

◇◇◇◇◇◇◇◇◇◇

You know, I can't help agreeing with you, Angela, that this part with the depression is quite a downer. I also agree with you, Donna—I don't think he was really trying to play God with his own life. Still, depressed is depressed. Sure he wanted to go home, and I can't really blame him given the situation, but I guess I still feel that we shouldn't necessarily excuse this much negativity.

Now, far be it from me to judge Piper on his attitude when I haven't been where he was. I'm just saying that this chapter is one heck of a depressing read. And, not to go making unfair comparisons, but have any of you read *Hope Beyond Reason* by Dave Hess? He was in the hospital for months with acute myeloid leukemia—a different situation, I know, but my point is that he suffered too, and almost as unexpectedly.

Now, Dave Hess had his rough times too. But his story on the whole is one saturated with hope and faith, and it makes for a much more uplifting and encouraging read. I found it so encouraging to read about how he loved the Lord in the midst of his pain, and how he positively interacted with and affected many of the hospital staff and other patients. He just kept on ministering God's love, no matter where he was!

I don't mean to judge Don Piper for his depression. All I'm saying is that, in all honesty, this chapter bummed me out big time, and this book has been a rough read ever since we returned to earth.

Your Reflections

_____

_____

_____

_____

_____

_____

_____

_____

_____

_____

_____

_____

_____

_____

_____

_____

_____

I Want to Go Back

CHAPTER 9

GIFTS AND HORSES

Shae

◇◇◇◇◇◇◇◇◇◇

"Don't look a gift horse in the mouth," so goes the ancient proverb! They say you can see a horse's age by its teeth. I'm looking a little long in the tooth, don't you think? Ha! Don wanted to do everything himself, and could not see the value of or the miracle of the great gift of  people God sent his way. These ones were an extension of God's hand and His love, and yet Don dismissed them in his heart, picking them like wasps from a cream jug.

Another Jewish saying goes, "Pride is the mask of one's own

faults." I am a great giver but a bad receiver, which falls into the category of selfishness too. Heaven help me if people should think me weak or of feeble faith. How could anyone know but me what was best for me? When my world fell apart, people offered to help, but I shushed, waved, and even swatted them away until...that cloak of iron befell me, and I buckled and could not help myself anymore. I believe this is how we can be still and know that God is God in the midst of our circumstances—through people interceding for us, pleading for us, standing in the gap for us, carrying the stinger, stinging us to humility, or even bearing the sting, in Christ-like love. The good news is...I can spot a good wasp from a bad wasp from a hundred yards I have become a horse person, transformed from a *neigh*-sayer to a yea-sayer...(groan).

Donna

◇◇◇◇◇◇◇◇◇◇◇

Don Piper's book is amazing, but his is not a story that easily lends itself to lightheartedness. Nor should it. The man has been to hell—make that Heaven—and back and has endured untold agonies since. That said, there's a humorous side to every situation and I'm about to collide with one.

Lest I offend, let me restate my position: Piper's situation was *not* funny. Neither was my cancer treatment, but I enjoyed the daily belly-laugh God afforded to get through the ordeal. And was it ever effective—especially when I looked in the mirror and saw a bald version of my dad staring back at me!

Anyway, this chapter sparked a serious-minded exploration of how it would feel to be bedridden for endless months. The idea of not being able to move is flat-out horrifying. The circumstance is fraught with medical perils; bedsores and pneumonia are serious business. And the cruel monotony! Staring at the ceiling gets old fast. I can get depressed just thinking about it.

But then I pictured *myself* flat on my back for 13 months. I quickly realized some of the less *traumatic*, but potentially *dramatic* implications. For one thing, I would have needed an adjustable-width bed. Are you kidding me? I could pack on an extra pound missing a single trip to the dryer. And the expression *bad hair day?* Well, it would take on a whole new meaning. I've seen myself after a mere eight hours in a prone position and it ain't pretty. (Ask the ladies with whom I attended last year's retreat.)

As the Bible says, *"A merry heart does good, like medicine..."* (Prov. 17:22 NKJV). My guess is that, even during his awful depression, Don Piper enjoyed moments of comic relief. I hope so....

Angela
◇◇◇◇◇◇◇◇◇◇◇

OMG Shae! Your horsey—LOL! And the adjustable-width bed, Donna...I'm there. In fact, I was thinking of this book as I was laying flat on my back in the dental hygienist's chair yesterday for the semi-annual probing, poking, polishing, spitting, and flossing, I stared at the ceiling for $97 worth of 45 minutes. Let's go together and create ceiling art and market it to dentists, eh?

Tammy, I'm so glad you mentioned the book *Hope Beyond Reason* by Dave Hess. Now *that* is a book filled with tragedy *and* hope! I suppose it confirms that God created each of us uniquely. We react to situations differently, we perceive circumstances differently, we believe at different levels—we are as unique as our DNA. What a God we serve who knows us each so intimately that He can dole out blessings in situations that will make some soar and others sore.

I hope and pray that I glorify Him and am a blessing to others during the good *and* bad times.

Tammy
◇◇◇◇◇◇◇◇◇◇

Praise the Lord for a blunt, tough-love 80-year-old preacher! I can't think of anyone else who would have the gall to tell a man living with intense pain that he needed to get his act together. Yet what a difference that message made!

As a virtual "kid" in years, I'm reminding myself right now that the reproof of my elders is fantastically precious to me. Proverbs 15:5 (as well as a whole lot of other Proverbs) reminds me to wake up and pay close attention when those older and wiser have something to say to me. I owe them honor—even when it's only my grandparents and their same old questions, "Where's your boyfriend? When are you going to start dating? When are you going to get married?" I have to remind myself sometimes that it's not honoring to throw "Never! Ha!" right back at them, LOL.

The great thing about such reproof is that it's offered in love. Even my grandparents' nagging is only because they want so much to see me happy. And Jay Perkins went even further with Don Piper—he gave him a dose of wisdom and tough love, not just for Piper's sake, but for the sake of all those longing to minister their love to him.

Where in the world would we be without our elders? Lost, that's where!

Your Reflections

_____

_____

_____

_____

_____

_____

_____

_____

_____

_____

_____

_____

_____

_____

_____

_____

_____

_____

_____

_____

_____

_____

_____

_____

_____

_____

_____

_____

_____

_____

_____

_____

_____

CHAPTER 10

TESTIFY TO LOVE

Shae

OK, this is when depression *is* bad, when fear rears to dash *all* hope and vision and all we see are those giant ugly oysters. A teen might call them "parents," lol. Binder, dun dat, wasn't good! Ouch Chihuahua. I remember my hopeless situation. The fear of it made me want to die, period! Cease to exist altogether. It created a huge chasm between earth and Heaven for me.

Without vision, people perish. Don could not see himself whole. He saw people's lips move in encouragement, but all he heard was "blah, blah, blah." As he said, he wanted to *see* results. The absence of results intensified his physical and spiritual pain. But you know what? Though at the start of this chapter he seems to have lost sight of Heaven, I see it all the more so, as a river of the water of life, as clear as crystal, flowing in and through his circumstances. Critics of this book cite their disappointment that there is not more of an account of Heaven in his story, but every page is like a flowing tributary of the river that flows from the very throne of God, thus we know that breakthrough is imminent and certain. And *voila*, joy broke through first.

Don was more disappointed with himself than he was with God. We don't all get to pop in and out of Heaven as he did, as he noted, but we cannot beat ourselves up when the cloak of heaviness befalls us either. It is then when we truly deplete ourselves of ourselves, and God fills us with wholeness, becoming perfect pearls not created by our circumstances, but by God's own heart and hand. Sure, when I am 80, I might *look* and feel like an oyster, but my countenance, pearlescent nevertheless in my expectation of soon being with God on a face-to-face basis. Woman, prepare to meet thy Maker. Ooh-la, and la!

Donna

◇◇◇◇◇◇◇◇◇◇◇

Yay! Another miracle—the return of joy! And with God's joy comes strength! (See Nehemiah 8:10.)

The dam of Don Piper's pent-up rage burst—or more accurately—was demolished in those pre-dawn hours in his hospital room. And what did God use as His divine wrecking ball? Music! The Father knew just how to penetrate Don Piper's heart. He knew Piper was a man who would not accept help and could not bare his emotions to others. So God unleashed the power of music in the middle of the night when no one was around but Don the son and his heavenly Dad.

A few simple lines about freedom; a melody to deliver the praises of the Christ and—smash!—like the walls of Jericho, the parapets around Don Piper's heart crumbled. The man with the mangled body and tortured soul no longer needed to act strong. Instead, he freely wept and allowed himself to be strengthened, not through determination or device, but through the divine nurture of unconditional love. In a moment's time, the rhythm of his life changed; as the music released truth into the atmosphere, Don Piper released himself and his emotions into God's able care. No longer his own shepherd, Piper was free to rest in God. The hope of the weary warrior was renewed, in the midst of uncertainty!

It's as though Don Piper allowed himself to *feel* again. As he did, the burden of concealment lifted and, with it, the depression that once threatened to consume him.

Angela

◇◇◇◇◇◇◇◇◇◇◇

"If it was me, I'd be yelling" the nurse told her patient in the book. When I was in the labor room awaiting the delivery of my first daughter some 30 years ago there was no comfy chair for others to lounge in or soft lights or cute-baby wallpaper or even smiling nurses. Back then, visitors weren't allowed, the rooms had sterile white walls, blinding white lights, and scratchy white sheets on a cold metal bed. There I was. Alone. During the many hours of agony, two other women were wheeled in, plopped in the bed beside me, curtain pulled between us, and then they screamed out in pain. Then both were wheeled out to the delivery room. "Oh dear Lord God, I'm in so much pain now, I can't even imagine what's coming that will make me scream out like the others." Finally after 24 hours, some whimpering but no screaming, I was wheeled out to the delivery room, given a big dose of "please put me out of my misery" medication, and about four hours later was introduced to a healthy, beautiful miracle. Like Don, I'm no screamer.

Also like Don, I am one attuned to contemporary Christian music. I listen constantly—one of those people who has to have "background" noise—maybe because of my former life as a reporter in a busy newsroom? Current favorite artists include: Toby Mac, Donnie McClurkin, Out of Eden, Kirk Franklin, and of course Michael W. Smith. Listening to music with a good beat and words that honor the Lord is the best medicine...and is sure to make hearts merry! One of my all-time favorite songs is by Avalon, "Testify to Love." When granddaughter Izabella was baptized, the priest held her high above his head and dedicated her to God—a very dramatic and special moment. Just then the choir sang "Testify to Love"* and I thought I would melt under the presence of the

Holy Spirit! What a powerful testimony of His faithfulness to every generation. (*See Appendix for lyrics.)

Tammy

Let this be a lesson to me—don't *ever* procrastinate some holy communion time with the Lord for the sake of a television show! LOL, I think it's glaringly obvious here that *The Brady Bunch*, in spite of their uplifting hilarity at other times, did not have the spiritual power to lift Don Piper's depression.

Beautifully, it was music that did. His favorite part of Heaven became the catalyst for the end of Piper's depression, even in its weak-by-comparison earthly form. Is it any wonder that he would find such release in music, when the human heart is so "attuned to tunes"? After all, the greatest Musician made us in His image, and He crafted us to adore the songs He loves to sing to our souls.

When I've been depressed in my life, it has been downright strange how music can bring healing. Even though I'm a person deeply inclined to words, sometimes no amount of talking could drive the shadows away. No poetry could say just the right thing, no prayers could express the feelings and the need for relief. Yet a few chords of music—lyrics completely optional, at times—could send a wave of cool, calming peace over my spirit that could clean me out right down to my painted toenails and give me the gift of a new breath of life.

That's the Holy Spirit at work for sure, dwelling within and between the notes, humming a loving lullaby to our troubled souls.

Your Reflections

_____

_____

_____

_____

_____

_____

_____

_____

_____

_____

_____

_____

_____

_____

_____

CHAPTER 11

HOME SWEET HOME

Shae

Also recall, Tammy, Don singing when left for dead, and the Baptist preacher singing over him. The book is rife with the miraculous power of music. Yet sometimes, I'll admit, I sing a different tune. It is hard for me to imagine *myself* as one day becoming perfect, which is what we will be in Heaven; morally (yea!) and bodily (yoo-hoo!) perfect. The moral part of perfection is a progressive spiritual growth in Christ—a process in which I often fall short. Sometimes when the enemy deems it a heyday on Shae, failure's baggage seems heavier than it should, hence, *"If you only knew..."* as Don Piper felt after he returned home from the hospital and people remarked on his amazing endurance and courage. I am also inclined to add, "Don't mistake my blond hair for a halo quite yet...!" Slap me silly, duh, gently though, as did God to Don. "They are not applauding for you." Drastic spotlight shift. Fade Shae to black. Enter God, stage right.

The physical part of perfection will happen in the twinkling of an eye, but it is often confused as a process, especially to women of my ilk, verging on 50 and wondering where all the elasticity has gone! I fall far short of bodily perfection! Save for major cosmetic surgery, I do what I can to keep things from slipping south, but I realize, it is a given that this body will fail me. Time = droop. But we do have hope—that day-of-no-need for wrinkle creams, lip plumpers, boob jobs, dermabrasion, tummy tucks, cheek implants, acrylic nails, contact lenses, laser chin-hair removal, and booty lifts is coming! I wish someone would tell that to Cher, a walking implant who is over 60 now, and trying to look 20. I hardly recognize her anymore... bless her heart. Would that I put in that much pain, endurance, and effort for my inner transformation—people would not recognize me either, but in my case, that would be a good thing. In Don's case, it is a fabulous thing; he's a dead man walking, and a living answer to the prayers of a multitude, to the glory of God.

Tammy

Woo, I hear ya, Shae! I'm looking forward to that perfect

heavenly body—and not the cookie-cutter Western culture idea of perfection either (making a strong showing in any lineup of supermodels). I'm talking perfect as in *exactly what God intends for us.* And, of course, even better will be the perfection of our *spirits* in Him. It's definitely an encouragement, as we watch our bodies failing us more and more (groan), to remember that, if we're seeking Him, our spirits are only growing stronger and closer to what they will be when perfected.

It's an inverse relationship (math word alert!) that I'm slowly working through. Of course, sometimes things get sped up a bit for us, like Don Piper experienced. I'm sure he wasn't expecting the sudden havoc wreaked on his body. The good news? He really did learn some spirit-strengthening lessons through the experience. (Oh my gosh, the math works?)

As he returns to church, to the welcome of those who love him, he's demonstrating both. Physically, though he survived, he will never be the same again. But spiritually he has learned some amazing things about allowing others to minister to him (Don Patrol, anyone?). He's been forced to give up control to others, and in the process has learned more about the One who ultimately controls everything.

I'm absolutely grateful that he's choosing to share his story—gives me a chance to take some of his lessons to heart, hopefully without having to experience everything he did. That's a blessing that being in a community of believers offers, and you'll find me joining the crowd in giving God a standing ovation for that idea!

Angela

◇◇◇◇◇◇◇◇◇◇◇◇

What a beautifully simple example of a son's love for his father when he laid his head on Dad's chest for a moment after returning home from school. Most parents cherish these (fleeting) moments as life swooshes by so very quickly. It was wonderful to read that Don had a breakthrough at the end of Chapter 10 and is now moving forward in his quest to get some normalcy back into his life. The smile on the one twin's face is priceless—or at least worth 1,000 words (see page 113). And the Don Patrol is what Christianity is all about. People helping people in need.

When I worked for a Christian nonprofit organization that established hospitals in third world countries to help disabled children, I had the opportunity to attend a conference of faith-based organizations sponsored by the government (G.W. Bush era). I was stunned by the number of everyday people who were committed to helping the homeless in their community, the abused children in their neighborhood, the addicts on their streets. I mingled with young, old, black, white, brown, Catholic, Protestant, Hindu, sincere, caring, faith-filled people who genuinely wanted to make (and were making) a difference in the lives of others—for His glory alone. Although I didn't agree with the president on fiscal issues, it is a tribute to him that he initiated and supported these faith-based organizations that are actually schlepping boxes and cans into the food banks, collecting blankets for cold families, wiping the noses of crying children, and hugging teenagers through withdrawal.

God bless the Don Patrols!

Donna
◇◇◇◇◇◇◇◇◇◇◇

God bless them, indeed! And, in Don Piper's case, thank God for those who constructed the ramp, removed the seat from the van, and handled all the other details involved with getting Piper back to church after his accident. It was a family affair—a veritable assembly line of compassion! Everyone contributed because a member of the family *needed* them.

Even geese are wired by their Maker to care for one another. I remember learning that, when a flock of geese travels, an amazing protocol takes over to ensure the group's progress and safety. Example: if one goose becomes hurt or ill and cannot fly, two members of the flock will drop out of formation and tend to their injured comrade.

The South Park "geese" descended upon the wounded member of their flock. What an undertaking it was on that "first" Sunday. And, after months away from church, I'm sure Don Piper found the attention of so many helpers on a single morning overwhelming—especially while dealing with the internal issues that no doubt surfaced that day. After all, he was returning to his church a changed man; the last time he'd been there Don Piper was a guy who seemingly had it all "under control."

If ever he needed to fellowship and worship with others, it was after his accident. I imagine it was a prime opportunity to emerge from the cocoon of self-preservation and self-focus that is automatically spun in the wake of incapacitating physical trauma. In some ways, it must have seemed a welcome chance to recover a sweet piece of "normalcy."

Your Reflections

_____

_____

_____

_____

_____

_____

_____

_____

_____

_____

_____

_____

_____

_____

_____

_____

CHAPTER 12

WHAT WOULD WE DO WITHOUT FRIENDS?

Donna

◇◇◇◇◇◇◇◇◇◇

We all need at least one David Gentiles in our lives. What a stellar example of a godly friend he is. No wonder Don Piper felt safe with him. He is the kind of person who loves people enough to accept them as they are, yet is willing to risk the pushback that comes when the truth is spoken in love. Not content to placate his friend by telling him what he wanted to hear, Gentiles walked the extra mile and became a willing part of God's plan to restore Don Piper and others through him. Fulfilling that role always comes at a price; it smokes both parties out of their respective comfort zones. And, although the give-and-take is glorious, the process is rarely tidy.

But oh is it worth it! I am *so* blessed to enjoy such friendships. I don't know where I'd be without the David Gentiles-types in my life. Time and again, God has shown Himself strong, loving, merciful, precise, generous, and knowable through these friendships. In His perfect economy, He causes these relationships to work both ways, always bringing fruit to bear in both lives—and in unforeseen and unimaginable ways.

Seen from my side of the equation, amazingly perceptive and grounded folks have sharpened my dullness (thank God for induced "aha moments,") sanded my jagged places (that'll cost ya), prodded me forward (irresistible force meets temporarily immovable object), called me to account (who me???), focused my attentions ("Ethel to Tillie...") inspired me (found a way through the concrete), and comforted me (when I needed it most).

The last time a friend profoundly affected my life and future? Just last night. And God was there. Big time.

Angela

I agree, Donna. What would we do without friends? Those with whom we can talk about the good, bad...and ugly. Speaking of which—a couple of friends dropped by unexpectedly the other night and we chatted in the kitchen over tall glasses of ice-cold water (I gave up caffeine a few years ago much to the surprise of friends and family). The topic—for them—turned to aches and pains as most conversations do these days I've noticed.

The verse at the beginning of Chapter 12 made me LOL when reading it and remembering what my friends said about their sore knees, big-jointed fingers, failing eyesight, thinning hair, and so on. "...We grow weary in our present bodies, and we long for the day when we will put on our heavenly bodies like new clothing....Our dying bodies make us groan and sigh, but it's not that we want to die and have no bodies at all. We want to slip into our new bodies so that these dying bodies will be swallowed up by everlasting life" (2 Cor. 5:1-4 NLT).

These friends happen to be 10 years older than I am so, oh joy, I have all these things to look forward to—not. But oh how glorious that day will be when we can shed these deteriorating bodies and "slip into our new bodies"! I wonder, Shae, if these new bodies will need shoes? ;)

Shae

Drum roll please. I have decided I want to go barefoot in Heaven. You know, tiptoe through the tulips with Jesus. Talk about transformation!

I am glad that Dave wisely counseled Don about his time in Heaven and if he should go public with it. At the outset of the story, I surmised the revealing of Heaven's graces to Don was for the tangible hope he would have to cling to for the hell ahead. I wasn't sure he was meant to share about the experience. God often tailors such things to and for the individual. For instance, why Don did not see Jesus is a mystery.

God knows, but some critics are trying to discount the experience as hallucination.

The world has discredited many great men and women of God who have revealed things perhaps meant for another time or place, for a specific person or group of people, or not at all. I know of one such evangelist mercilessly and publicly lambasted by pharisaic police, and ridiculed by media for revealing a pretty far out vision he had. Then again, sometimes I just have to say the word, "Jesus," and all hell breaks loose! Talk about pushback, as Donna termed it. More like, "back off!" The risk is not for the faint of heart or overly sensitive but it is helpful to remember what someone once said, "All that is necessary for evil to triumph is for good [people] to do nothing."

It took courage and resolve, conviction and buckets of love to counsel my best friend "Cindy," who was battling depression, anxiety, and a host of personal problems, that she should try Jesus. Lord knows, she had tried everything else: doctors, narcotics, crystals, auras, and the goddess within. "...Try Jesus...just try Him...." I haven't heard from her since.

Tammy
◇◇◇◇◇◇◇◇◇◇◇

It's the absolute truth. We have the Answer, the one and only Way to eternal life instead of eternal death. How can we claim to love *anyone* if we're willing to stand by and watch them merrily walk away from Him? What kind of a friend am

I if I don't tell the ones I claim to care about how to find the truth their souls are dying for?

The answer is: a horrible friend. And I have been guilty of being exactly that far too often. (Tragic, but true.) I have allowed fear to shut my mouth like evil duct tape, I have allowed peer pressure to sway my behavior, I have listened to friends profess their belief in lies and said nothing true in return. For all these moments of self-centered failure, I can only repent and pray that God will still use me as His hands and feet. And He does, thankfully.

I've also had moments when, by His grace, I managed to be a true friend. I can relate to your experience, Shae—it hasn't always resulted in the most welcoming response from those I reached out to. Yet, at the same time, I have faith that the Lord will use our obedience even if we never see the fruit. "As the rain and the snow come down from Heaven, and do not return to it without watering the earth...so is My Word that goes out from My mouth: It will not return to Me empty, but will accomplish what I desire and achieve the purpose for which I sent it" (Isa. 55:10-11).

I think I'll give myself a dare today: pray for God to show me someone I can be a *true* friend to, and then *do it*.

Your Reflections

_____

_____

_____

_____

_____

_____

_____

_____

_____

_____

_____

_____

_____

_____

_____

What Would We Do Without Friends?

_____

_____

_____

_____

_____

_____

_____

_____

_____

_____

_____

_____

_____

_____

CHAPTER 13

HAND IN HAND

Shae

Ho! What a thrilling revelation to learn that the hand that held yours when confronted with the depth and darkness of pain and death, belonged to a divine being. But I wonder, could it not have been God's own hand that clasped Don's? How did he conclude the hand belonged to an angel? Perhaps the recollection of the Scripture about entertaining angels unaware confirmed it for him. Yet he was definitely not entertaining them. I guess it doesn't really matter. God calls upon the angels to minister, guide, provide, protect, deliver, comfort, gather, and to save His elect from accidents or premature death as extensions of His hand, in much the same way they ministered to Jesus in the desert and strengthened Him in the Garden in His humanity. But I was a little let down that Jesus wasn't there in Person, no disrespect to the angel. Am I a spoiled princess or what? *grin* Hey, I just want my hand in the hand of *the* Man, period. That said, I know of instances in my own life where angels *have* intervened, comforted, and saved me, and I am grateful!

I shudder to think how much worse Don Piper's situation would have been with no awareness of God. The most terrible anguish would be to have to bear such pain without any sense of the nearness of God's love. To cry out in fear and to hear no reply, or to reach out in the darkness for a hand to hold onto and to find no hand offered, or to call out in agony at the eleventh hour and hear no words of comfort, are fearful forsaking thoughts. There was a hand there holding his—not the Hand of Jesus, per se, but a heavenly hand, nevertheless. In hindsight, I would be OK with that. Um, more than OK.

Tammy

God sends His angels to comfort and assist us. He sent one to save my life when I was three years old.

My mom was traveling by train, alone...and she was five months pregnant with my little sister. She'd gone from Baltimore to Grand Central Station in New York City with a three-year-old in tow (me), an eleven-month-old on her hip, and a month's worth of luggage for all of us. She was going to stay at her sister-in-law's, and someone was supposed to meet her at Grand Central. She couldn't find that person anywhere.

Finding a pay phone, she called my aunt—you can imagine, I'm sure, the state she was in. She didn't even notice when I wandered off...straight for the train tracks. If it hadn't been for an angel, she says, Tammy may have died that day.

Instead, a complete stranger appeared beside me, took me by the hand, and walked me right over to my mom, mysteriously knowing exactly who I belonged to without being told. This person handed me off to my mom, smiled, and walked away, disappearing into the crowd. Mom says she just knew it was an angel.

Praise the Lord for sending His messengers when we need someone to hold our hand.

Angela

Since we're sharing our angelic thoughts and experiences...I woke up when I was five years old and saw an angel standing beside my bed. I felt peaceful and there was a beautiful feeling of love between us. (See Matthew 18:10.) Then the angel faded away. The next morning I told my mother about the angel, and she just smiled and nodded. I realize now that her response was the best. No scoffing, no inquisition, just a smile and a nod. My mother was wonderful that way.

My oldest daughter and her best friend were in a tragic car accident years ago. The driver of a van crashed into the back of their small car as they were stopped to make a turn (with the turn signal on). I have often thought that God immediately sent an angel (or two) to comfort and hold her friend's hand those last few moments of earthly life and how He welcomed her into His everlasting Kingdom of love and joy in Heaven. He and His angels of mercy are always on duty—hugging us when we need a boost of energy, cheering us on when we're weary, holding our hand when we need a friend. And I have no doubt that angels more than once came to the aid of our youngest daughter whose free spirit and strong will led her to South Philly, Italy, Hawaii, California, and then New York City, where she finally completed her five-year, five-college undergraduate career.

There was a photo today on the Web of President Obama and his wife holding hands as they took a stroll outside the White House. Hand holding is sweet, kind, and a gentle, intentional way of telling someone that they are cared for, loved, nice to be near—touchable.

If only for a moment, hold someone's hand today.

Donna
◇◇◇◇◇◇◇◇◇◇◇

There's something about the touch of one hand on another. It's so deeply personal, so expressive that words are unnecessary. The emotional vocabulary is universal. I've seen it spoken fluently in those popular greeting cards and ad campaigns in which an adult hand holds a tiny, dimpled infant hand.

Who needs words? Beginning, middle, and end of story are easily imagined. Instantly, a smile erupts. Most "readers" are moved to reminiscence or tears or both. In a millisecond, the subconscious has filled in any blanks with words such as *safety, security, comfort, guidance...and deep, abiding, preserving love.*

As I read about Anita's correction to Don Piper's story, I took the same gleeful road Shae did. Wow. God was there, making His presence known in a dark place, taking His boy's hand in His own in the most consequential of moments.

Makes me wonder whether He held my hand as I tumbled in the womb or as I exited that watery world and entered this one. (I hope He was holding Mom's hand as she labored!) I wonder if He'll hold my hand as I leave this life and return home to Him.

Somehow, I think so. In fact, I'm sure of it.

Your Reflections

_____

_____

_____

_____

_____

_____

_____

_____

_____

_____

_____

_____

_____

_____

_____

_____

_____

Hand in Hand

CHAPTER 14

SEEING NORMAL

Shae

It is good if you can believe it, and I believe it! Wow on these angelic, divine encounters, but nothing tops salvation in the realm of the miraculous. I mean, think of it, we beat *death* and its *sting*, and get to hang out with Jesus forever, in the manner in which God intended all along, naturally normal, the way He created humanity before the fall of Adam and Eve without the need to adjust or accept physical limits as Don Piper has had to do. The angels know how profound salvation is, and have been singing its praises since they saw normal created in the Garden of Eden, Christ born in a manger, and a troubled, lost teen fall to her knees and surrender all to Jesus. I am telling you, I am a walking example of one supernaturally natural makeover! Oh, and I still feel like a teen to the cha-grin of my 13 year old. But my liver spots give me away.

The account of Don's twin sons and his daughter being sent to live with extended family touched a chord with me. My twin brother and I and my five elder siblings were sent away a number of times when my mother was too ill to care for us, and simply could not cope. In my case I was the cool but sensitive one and didn't show my feelings as easily as my brother did, who tended to act them out mischievously. I don't know that I felt cheated out of normal at the time, I was just scared. The last time we left, we never returned home. Later, as a teen, I acted out in rebellion, but when I came to know Jesus, I did not feel cheated at all because He showed me in a vision how very near He was to me, through everything. Today I see all the good wrought out of the bad and the sad, and I am glad! *doing a touchdown dance for the Lord.*

Angela

◇◇◇◇◇◇◇◇◇◇◇

Gee, Shae, I'm sorry that you had to go through all that as a child, but like you said, God was with you every step of the way. PTL! I'm continually amazed at how God provides for us in the most benevolent of ways—He nourishes us physically, mentally, spiritually. I agree with the author, "We tend to forget the negative and go back to recapture pleasant events." So true that our minds were created in such a way that we can allow the unpleasant memories to fade away and enjoy the "good old days." These days I like to remember our daughters' teenage years not for the rebellious and hormone-crazed trials and tribulations, but for the night one was inducted into the National Honor Society and the other for the standing ovations after thrilling performances on stage. I choose to remember the times when we actually sat at the dinner table together and chatted about our days, the fun times at Hershey Park, Disney World, and our crazy vacation to Barbados. I love to re-read the little notes and homemade cards they made me and Daddy for special occasions.

The choices we make every day affect others as well as ourselves. Don Piper's wife had to make some life-changing choices for her husband. That would be a very hard thing to do. Very hard. I'm glad he finally talked more about her in Chapter 14. My heart went out to her from the very first chapter when she first received the call about her husband's accident. How terrifying that must have been for her. I think she should write a book about how she maintained a semblance of normalcy when her world was falling apart. I'd love to hear her side of the story.

Tammy

I'm with you, Angela! I've actually wondered about Eva's side of the story several times throughout the book so far. We get some glimpses of it here, finally, as well as a tiny bit told in her own words. I must say, this lady is one tough cookie! To handle working, making all those decisions, and constantly being at the hospital, and then after that, caring for her husband at home all the time—and even Don Piper admits he wasn't the best patient—she amazes me. And in the midst of all that, a nurse actually refused to tell her something about her husband's condition, telling her she was "just a wife"! What? "Just" nothing! Looks to me like she was the glue that kept everything from truly falling apart.

I try to imagine being in her shoes, and I'm pretty sure I wouldn't do as well. If I had a convalescing husband who nit-picked everything I did, I'd probably blow a Tammy-gasket, not be happy, and take it as a sign of recovery. On top of that, holding my tongue has never been a particularly strong forte of mine. Good thing I didn't even attempt a career in nursing—I'd have failed miserably in "Bedside Manner"!

Don Piper was blessed to receive the help and encouragement of many people...and even angels! But among those supporters on this side of Heaven, I'm absolutely amazed and inspired the most by Eva. What a grace-filled daughter of the Lord!

Donna

◇◇◇◇◇◇◇◇◇◇◇◇

Oh, yes! Eva is really something! Good thing, too, because she had a ton on her plate after the accident. From where the rest of us sit, she certainly sounds like a woman with the gumption to plow through and get an impossible job done.

As I write those words, the Holy Spirit reminds me that there is no Homeland-Security-style dry run for personal catastrophes like the one suffered by the Pipers. We don't come to unimaginable situations with a perfectly-honed sense of preparedness and a remote control for its instant deployment. Instead, we develop a contingency here and a scheme there: exit plans in case of fire; insurance to indemnify against untoward events; a rainy-day fund for who knows what. It's all good, but when you're unexpectedly splayed out at Your Personal Ground Zero, it's never enough.

Eva's "gumption" was bigger than any contingency plan. Moment by moment, it morphed into whatever she needed it to be: *strength, peace, comfort, patience, compassion, more strength, more peace, more comfort, more patience, more compassion.* What she had going for her was not really "gumption"; it was the grace of God. How else could she face the unknown realms of The New Normal? It was a balancing act of absurd proportions: watch your husband suffer through pain and depression; shoulder his everyday responsibilities; juggle the new routines every crisis generates; go to work each day—and, if you don't mind, do all of it simultaneously until further notice.

Life must have looked like floodwaters as far as the eye could see...a series of adjustments that is probably ongoing even today. Which is what makes His grace so undeniably cool—the Pipers pulled off the impossible and are arguably more productive than ever!

Your Reflections

_____

_____

_____

_____

_____

_____

_____

_____

_____

_____

_____

_____

_____

_____

_____

_____

_____

CHAPTER 15

DOOHICKEYS

Shae

The Bible inspires us with many confidence-boosting words of encouragement and promises that are easy enough to believe in until we have to cash them in and apply them to our present circumstances, whether extreme, as Don's were, or mild. To put, "all things work together for the good..." to the test when one's life is a living hell is not easy. I have trouble enough holding on to the good if I am under the dentist's drill or have a bad hair day!

I agree with Angela's Chapter 14 post, our choices affect others. It took an act and attitude of Don's will to trust God to *deliver* the good *from* the bad, and for peace and joy to return to his life and family, not a dependence upon emotions or feelings. It would have been a great mistake had he basked in misery and chosen otherwise, thus missing the divine promise and assurance of good outcomes. Where would his faith be? More shattered than his bones. Where would that grouch in the leg doohickey be? Six feet under. The unbelieving dying woman? "Down there" too. Don's wife? At the lawyers. Me? Probably toothless, bald, and still whining.

Angela

"Doohickey"—I haven't heard that term for eons! Thanks for the flashback, Shae. There are lot of doohickey-type things in life. Things that make us uncomfortable, things we don't want to admit, things that help us grow, go, or groan. Who can deny that God puts people in the right place at the right time? Well, I suppose people can disagree with the truth, but I believe that God arranges the arrangements, plans the plan, and situates the situations. He knew who needed (and needs) to hear the author's story. He knows the hearts that will be softened and turned toward Him after hearing about Don's trip to Heaven. God knows all about the doohickeys in our lives that need to be screwed more tightly to get our attention.

Every time I get too comfortable in my career, relationships, spiritual life, family circumstance, etc., God comes along and tightens the screw. I eventually (I'm a slow learner) feel the pinch to make improvements in this or that area, to make amends with this or that person, to consider this or that opportunity. It's way too easy to get in a rut or become a slave to a routine and miss all that God has provided. Wake up and feel the doohickey!

Tammy

Haha, Shae, I LOL when I read you referring to the fixator as a doohickey...and my cat woke up and gave me a look from my lap. "Nothing funny about a doohickey," he seemed to say.

Well sure, Kitty—lesson-teaching doohickeys can be miserable, and they don't have to cause excruciating physical pain either. Just take a look at any good, strong relationship. Other people are tons of fun, but they invariably also prove excellent screw-tighteners when we open up to them. I bet that between the prompting of the Holy Spirit and the ever-present hands of the people in our lives, we feel the twist or pull of our own personal doohickeys every day.

But hey, even if the lesson hurts at the time, does that have to mean we can never laugh about it? I wouldn't say so. I love to laugh over the once-horrific lessons that tempered my selfishness (a little), my bluntness (some), and my pride (a lot, but not nearly enough yet). I have known other people, currently experiencing the twist of lessons much like my past ones, to take encouragement from seeing me as a picture of their future—doohickey-free. Don Piper also presented himself as such a picture to more than one person suffering the fixator. Of course, in that situation, laughing at the torture of the fixator would not be helpful, but my point is that a positive attitude about such things can be a cheering ray of hope to others.

Besides that, it's just plain *funny* to see how God stretches us to grow in life sometimes. ^_^

Angela

Oh no! Not the doohickey!

Have you ever noticed how, at certain times, all the doohickeys get tightened at once?

What's up with that? And isn't it illegal? Whether a series of random events causes all the screws to turn at once (Exhibit "A" for *Ahora*) or one errant doohickey causes a chain reaction on the Highway of Life (Exhibit "B" for *Been there, done that*) doesn't really matter. Critical mass is just not the place I want to be. So can somebody please tell me why I didn't get to sign-off on this out-of-whack itinerary?

OK, so my hyperbolic rant is well, hyperbolic. But it *feels* accurate. A family crisis here *(Say, what?)*; an involuntary move from the third floor there *(You have to renovate my apartment by when?)*; surgery needed to reverse the effects of surgery *(Trust me; that will have to wait.)*; the divine de-feathering of a well-constructed and comfortable "nest" *(Hey, Bubba, I built that thing to last!)*; and the rewiring of a mindset or two *(And what did You say would happen when we pull out those pick-up sticks?)*.

If you ask me, my doohickeys are trying to kill me. But, I have to admit, they crack me up too. They remind me how fluid life is and how rigid I can be even when I'm swearing up and down that my middle name is *Gumby*.

A quick look in the rear-view mirror brings it all into focus and reminds me that I *have* been here before...and God has always made premium lemonade out of my measly lemons: :)

Your Reflections

_____

_____

_____

_____

_____

_____

_____

_____

_____

_____

_____

_____

_____

_____

_____

_____

_____

_____

_____

_____

_____

_____

_____

_____

_____

_____

_____

_____

_____

_____

_____

_____

_____

_____

CHAPTER 16

BOUGHT THE T-SHIRT

Shae

Don struggled to find purpose again in being alive, especially after popping into the light and back. What a contrast and even more reason why I am confused that his purpose was not immediately evident to him, especially since God deemed it necessary to return him to earth. His was a testimony few people have. I mean, he is right up there with Peter, Paul, Ezekiel, Isaiah, Mary, Enoch, the biblical greats! Perhaps Don was coming from the husband/father/provider POV because I believe that he knew his calling: Tell people about the hope of Heaven and eternal life. Which he did. Encourage them to live well. Which he did. Persuade the brokenhearted that there is comfort where there are no answers, in that God never leaves or forsakes us, on earth or in Heaven. Which he did. And, proclaim though we have to live with less than perfect now, it won't be forever. Which he did, and continues to proclaim brilliantly. Some people will believe Heaven is real only when they see it, and they may miss eternity with God.

But there are some who will settle for the testimony of a tangible person who has been there and back, and to that end, Don Piper is the man of the hour, called to do just that. Lord, me next!

Angela

◇◇◇◇◇◇◇◇◇◇

Like you, Shae, I was glad to read that the author was finally facing his purpose and sharing his story. His story changed people's lives. It seemed so obvious to me throughout the book that he should have been sharing his experience, but then again hindsight is 20/20, right? Who's to say that people looking at my life aren't shaking their heads and thinking, *Dah, gee, why isn't she doing* _____ (I'd fill in the blank if I had a clue).

I believe that comforting others who are going through the same type of situations we have gone through is one of the reasons we have had those experiences. God knows we need each other to get through tough times and to rejoice with through good times. I've been an encourager for moms who have had challenging times with their teenage daughters. I've been a listener for friends whose parents have passed away.

I've been a motivator for those having career setbacks. I've been a congratulator for new parents and grandparents. Through it all, our heavenly Father provides others who can relate—they've already bought the t-shirt. Of course if no one is around, always remember that Jesus has a closet full of all the t-shirts ever made.

Tammy

Don Piper described the "fixator club" to the cop, Brad, as a "small fraternity" that none of them had exactly been jumping to get into.

Now I'm not in that fraternity and I can only thank the Lord for that. But as I look at my life, I can identify the clubs and fraternities (or sororities, if you like) that I've been in. I didn't jump to join any of mine either. (Angela, you too— that's a lot of clubs you've been in, and I'm willing to bet you didn't ask for any of them!) But the good news is, once you're in, you've got a ministry to your frat brothers and sorority sisters for life.

I'm no counselor, but sometimes a kid doesn't want to talk to one about their depression. Sometimes it helps just to feel a hug from someone in the same club who can tell you with conviction that it's not the end of the world. I'm not a doctor, either, but there comes a point for a person who is losing a family member to cancer when explanations from doctors just don't help anymore. Even if I can't tell them, "It'll be

OK," in such a situation, being able to hear, "I know it hurts," is sometimes all we need.

Piper was able to share those words with quite a few people, even though it's never easy to open up and be honest about our pain. Yet, for the sake of our brothers and sisters, I hope none of us will ever back down from an opportunity to stand with other people in our "clubs" of suffering and encourage them through their trial.

Donna

There is no doubt we get signed up for clubs we never asked to join. And I agree that when we go through times of trial or trauma, we often make divinely-appointed connections with other "club" members who *get it*.

Since my twenties, I have lost many friends and several loved ones to cancer. As they pressed through their ordeals, I tried to be as supportive as possible, knowing they were intimately acquainted with a level of suffering for which I had no frame of reference. All I could do was love them the best way I knew how.

Then I joined the club. Of the many friends and loved ones who had joined before me, only two from my inner circle were still alive. One was 2,000 miles away. The other, Karen, lived in Denver, as I do. She encouraged me and did wonderfully loving things for me. Very near the end of her life, she packed a carton with all the ingredients needed for a gourmet lunch (including a floral arrangement!) and then prepared the feast at my house so it would be fresh. What a sweet time it was.

Karen and I shared many experiences common to cancer patients. That commonality was helpful to both of us. Yet I felt it was important for me to remember that our individual paths were also unique. I could not base my prospects and hopes for the future on the outcomes other "club" members had already experienced. I had to live my life according to the grace and guidance God was giving me...and I had to do it one day at a time.

I'm thankful for the undying love of my fellow "club" members...and comforted with the thought that they are whole and sound in Heaven.

Your Reflections

_____

_____

_____

_____

_____

_____

_____

_____

_____

_____

_____

_____

_____

_____

_____

_____

_____

_____

Bought the T-shirt

CHAPTER 17

"WOULDN'T IT BE LOVERLY"

Shae

I have a question about Don's heavenly greeting committee. He says, on page 196, "They're still there at the gate…. they're waiting." Which side of the gate? Still on the outside? Waiting for who/what, me? Break down the door people! Hey, I want "in" where God is. Or am I *missin' sumpin'*? Hopefully Heaven isn't about loitering at the gate waiting for loved ones when we could be inside enjoying all that God has prepared for us. You know, running barefoot with Jesus…exploring the mansions, all that stuff. I mean you can only stare at humongous pearls for *so* long.

Angela

◇◇◇◇◇◇◇◇◇◇

That is puzzling to me as well, Shae. I've always envisioned my loved ones waiting for me on the front porch of their mansions (see John 14:2) as I stroll down golden streets hand in hand with Jesus. "Oh look! It's Angela and Jesus! We're so glad to see you! Come up and sit for a while...an everlasting while!" And time will be no more. No more hurrying to get to the dentist's office on time. No more worrying about banking hours. No more keeping track of hair appointments or driving to the market before it closes for that missing ingredient. No more rushing to and from work each day. Oh, won't it be so "loverly"!

As many people have said many times, we are not promised tomorrow so live for today. That concept can be taken many different ways, but I prefer it to mean appreciate today's blessings. Tally them up before you get out of bed and before you close your eyes at night. Someone in a prayer group admonished us to list 10 things in our minds that we are thankful for before we get out of bed each morning. Most mornings I remember. The love of my Savior and His sacrifice for me always tops the list. Depending on what's going on in my life, the other nine thanks are random ranging from my husband and my work to my pillow and my dog. We (Americans especially) are blessed beyond imagination...ask any little girl or boy in Haiti or Darfur, for example. How many times have they longed for a heavenly home where there is always food to eat, clean water to drink, and more than enough love for everyone.

Tammy

Sometimes I have to remind myself that Don Piper's view of death (and mine) is a little abnormal in this world, to say the least. Throughout history it has been common for humans to fear death as a threatening unknown. What a different perspective we are privileged to have, knowing what waits for us and being free to happily anticipate it!

What's more, in Piper's case, he can actually *remember* Heaven. He knows it's a real place because he saw it and tasted the very fringes of eternal joy. I know it's a real place through faith, but I'm in the "no eye has seen" category (see 1 Cor. 2:9). Either way though, death takes on a whole new look to us—not a frightening end, but an exciting beginning. Not a dread unknown, but a thrilling promise—one Piper is anticipating daily, as I'm sure we all are too, my Powder Room sisters.

Death, where is your sting, indeed? Even the sting of loss dissipates into rejoicing for those who have the confident joy of knowing that their departed loved ones are, at this very moment, experiencing His rapturous, undiluted love.

I just can't wait to see, hear, taste, and explore that "undiscovered country" on the arm of my divine Lover...forever.

Donna

Ahhh Heaven. Completion. Restoration. Pure, unadulterated

freedom. Unobstructed light and unrelenting worship. Every tear dried...every wound healed...every fear vanquished...every broken heart mended—seamlessly.

I'm with you, Shae. Once departed, I want inside those gates on the double...now! And as for my welcoming committee, I'm with you, Angela. Just let me stroll on up to their porches and rejoice with them there. And, Tammy, you described it so beautifully: "on the arm of my divine Lover." That's where I want to be!

Oh, I can feel His touch. I can taste the sweetness of the atmosphere. I sense the depths of endless joy. And—wait—do I detect the aroma of lasagna wafting from a particular heavenly porch?

Oh, what a homecoming!

Your Reflections

_____

_____

_____

_____

_____

_____

_____

_____

_____

_____

_____

_____

_____

_____

_____

_____

CHAPTER 18

IT IS HUMAN TO WONDER

Shae

Thanks to Don for letting us see into his thoughts somewhat. But I really want to pick Job's brain (and heart) when I get to Heaven. The man lost his children, his wife, his health, an empire, yet grew into a deeper relationship with God. Yikes, one stock market crash alone and people leap off tall buildings.

It is human to wonder why bad things happen, especially to good people; but for years, I would not ask God, "why," likely because of the counsel of well-meaning though superficially spiritual people. "Just accept that bad happened...we don't question God!" Clunk went the gavel and down shot the lightning bolt in my mind's eye view of Him. However, after I entered into a *relationship* with my Father in Heaven, my paradigm shifted as I discovered His *loving* character and approachability and felt freer to ask and even cry out those tough questions. Asking why even from a point of crazed desperation often led me to true prayer. Hey, I am His child; children ask "why" of their parents all day long. My son was a *why-ner!* It is precisely because I am in relationship with my heavenly Father that I have freedom to express my true feelings.

I may not see reasons why until I get to Heaven but I can live with mystery for now, as Job had to, as Don has, as you have, Donna, in your battle with cancer, and you, Tammy, in the pictures of your past, and Angela, with the challenges of growing a family. What Don saw was enough, such that he could say, "It will be worth it all...." What Job saw was *more than enough*, "My eyes see Thee." As long as I can see God, I know that my latter end will be more blessed than my beginning, as it was for Job. And, since God never leaves or forsakes us, that blonde you read about jumping off the Grand Canyon without a parachute, *won't* be me.

Angela

Job. Now there's a guy who loved his Lord. I've read and edited quite a few books about Job. And no doubt you've heard, "She (not referring to me in any way, shape, or form) has the patience of Job." Although God allowed satan to mess with Job, Job didn't allow satan to mess with the relationship he had with his heavenly Father. His faith went so deeply that he persevered through all the loss. Although Don shared (and shared and shared) his thoughts about his pain and wanting to go back to Heaven with his readers, he never doubted that His Lord and Heaven are real and that he will return to them some day.

There are aspects of life that we have to know that we have know are real. Not everything is "relative" or "compromisable." I may wonder from time to time about why this or that happened, or wonder if I'm making the right decision, or wonder what God is trying to tell me through a certain situation. But I don't wonder about my faith. I believe that Jesus Christ is the only Son of the Almighty God. Others may believe otherwise and that is their choice, but for me and my house, we will serve the Lord.

Tammy

◇◇◇◇◇◇◇◇◇◇

Isn't our God something else? Is there another being worshiped as a deity in this world who openly says to his followers, "Here I am; this is what I'm like, and this is what I do. Any questions? Complaints?" And then He actually *listens* to the endless "whys" of humanity and the seemingly infinite gripes of ones such as I—ever full of grace, He listens, yes, but even more, He *answers*. Does Allah welcome questions? Does Brahma actually answer those who ask? Nope and nope. In fact, this was the biggest thing that convinced me of our God's reality when I was seeking.

Me: "Hey God, are You real?"

God: "This is what I am like. Could you or any other human have invented Me?"

Me: "Hmmm...nope."

End of story. ^_^ I found that talking to Him, knowing that He loves me enough to hear and answer me, is quite the best thing on this planet. Yet it's gonna get even more amazing in Heaven, when we can walk hand in hand and communicate directly.

Have I said this before? I just can't wait!

Donna

◇◇◇◇◇◇◇◇◇◇

Nor can I. Nothing sounds better than eternity in Heaven. Nothing *could be* better.

Yet I haven't packed my bags just yet. My Lord healed me several years ago. Premature exit visa *cancelled*. I'm good with that. Heck—I'm thankful for it! Every day He gives me is one He has crafted with His own hands. May I drink from it every drop of His goodness and yield from it all the glory that is due Him. I know I will fall short, but His grace is sufficient (see 2 Cor. 12:9). I'm committed to His plan for the here and now, at least for here and now.

But I have a wandering eye; no matter what I'm doing or thinking, it darts upward to the place He has prepared for me. It's infinitely better than where I am now. And—oh—the features! Only the likes of Don Piper and the "permanently" departed have sampled those. Heaven is the only place *"where moths and rust cannot destroy, and thieves do not break in and steal"* (Matt. 6:20 NLT)...the only place where tears are forever dried and bodies are completely sound.

Alas, even my roving eye senses that there is more for me to learn and do before I exit this life and enter the next. Far be it for me to abbreviate His *now* plan. Today I will be satisfied with the riches of His presence in my life on earth. And, until I go, I will sing His praises and hope for those I meet to develop a wandering eye and accept the keys to the place He has prepared for them in Heaven.

I pray I'll see *you* there...someday.

Your Reflections

_____

_____

_____

_____

_____

_____

_____

_____

_____

_____

_____

_____

_____

_____

_____

_____

It Is Human to Wonder

EPILOGUE

Wow—I can't believe we've reached the end of analyzing, x-raying, examining, dissecting, probing, scrutinizing and thoroughly blogging to pieces another best-selling book together. The cover of the original *90 Minutes in Heaven* book boasts "More than 3 million copies sold" and I can only imagine that there are 3 million different opinions about it as well. The opinions we four shared came from the bottom of our hearts and the tips of our loafered, stiletto-toed, cowboy-booted, and tennis-shoed toes. Thank you for schlepping through it and life with us.

We've grown a lot reading what the others had to say, which is why it is so cool to listen and learn. The only time we stop learning is when we stop listening. The most important voice to listen for is that of your heavenly Father. His still small voice is calling you into a relationship with Him. His heart's desire is to bring you peace, joy, love, and eternal life.

We've enjoyed our time reflecting in the Powder Room of life—we hope you can say the same.

Your Reflections

_____

_____

_____

_____

_____

_____

_____

_____

_____

_____

_____

_____

_____

_____

_____

_____

_____

INVITATION

Have you ever wondered where you will be when you come to the end of your life? It doesn't take a 90 minute trip to Heaven to know that you can spend eternity there. God cares about you. You have God's word on it that you matter to Him. He loves you so much that He gave His only Son for you. If you are seeking more to this life, you may not know it, but you are seeking God; He meant for your life to be full. You can receive assurance of Heaven and Christ right now by faith through prayer. Prayer is simply talking to God, just as we in the Powder Room talk to each other. God knows your heart and is not as concerned with your words as He is with the attitude of your heart. If it is leaning toward Him, and this prayer expresses the desire of your heart, please pray it now.

Lord Jesus, I want to know You personally, to have the assurance of living forever with You and my loved ones in eternity. Thank You for dying on the Cross for my sins. I open the door of my life to You and ask You to come in as my Savior, and the Lord of my life. Take control of it all. I surrender it to You. Thank You for forgiving my sins and giving me eternal life. Make me into the person You want me to be. Amen.

If you have prayed this prayer, right on! Christ has come into your life, as He promised! We will see you in Heaven—what a day of rejoicing it will be! Whether you prayed this prayer or not, we also encourage you to read the Bible and seek the truth for yourself in God's Word. We are praying for you.

Your Reflections

_____

_____

_____

_____

_____

_____

_____

_____

_____

_____

_____

_____

_____

_____

_____

_____

_____

_____

_____

_____

_____

_____

_____

_____

_____

_____

_____

_____

_____

_____

_____

_____

_____

_____

Glossary

Anchors aweigh!—here we go, sailor!

Binder, dun dat—been there, done that

Bought the t-shirt—see binder, dun dat

BTW—By The Way

Bummed out—state of mind that sends a girl for her chocolate stash

Checked into the boards—a hockey euphemism for getting pasted onto the rink's perimeter by an opposing player

Country/Bluegrass—music that some people like

Don't even go there—That topic of discussion will cause a conversational U-ee (see U-ee)

Doohickey—doodad, gizmo, thingamabob, thingamajig, whatchamacallit

Dumbo—Disney's adorable little baby elephant with ears twice his size; proof that Disney can make *any* animal cuddly

Drudge Report—constantly updated national and international Internet news page from various sources; www.drudgereport.com

Freak out—what Tammy does when she sees a spider...or reads something *way* gross

Head-on living—Life 101, "The School of Hard Knocks" (headbutts with referred pain to the heart)

Hunkey dorey or hunky dory—everything is fine, OK, groovy

Jesus Freak—awesome song by DC Talk; bumper sticker my kids made fun of

lol—not short for "Lolita!" (laughing out loud)

LOL—LAUGH OUT LOUD loudly

Loverly—"Wouldn't It Be Loverly"; song from *My Fair Lady*

Ouch Chihuahua—a painful yelp

Octomom—single mom who gave birth to 8 babies in 2009; already had 6 children

PTL—Praise The Lord!

Schlepping—hoisting something; sometimes your feet when strolling in no particular direction

Sweats—clothing preferred for stay-at-home writers of every age, make, model

Swift kick in the pants—a blunt reminder, sans sugarcoating; a big "Hel-*lo*! Anybody home?"

TMI—Too Much Information; also Three Mile Island nuclear plant in Pennsylvania

Thingy—Shae's attempt at sounding techie. See doohickey

U-ee—slang for "U-turn" or "I brake for sales"

:P—sticking your tongue out at yourself

Volume to 11—a *Spinal Tap* phenomenon by which volume on a scale of 1 to 10 is magically maxed out at 11 instead

^_^—Tammy's smile. Just picture a halo over it

Your Reflections

_____

_____

_____

_____

_____

_____

_____

_____

_____

_____

_____

_____

_____

_____

_____

_____

_____

Your Reflections

APPENDIX

"Testify to Love" by Avalon
(Sparrow Records 2003)

All the colors of the rainbow
All the voices of the wind
Every dream that reaches out
That reaches out to find where love begins
Every word of every story
Every star in every sky
Every corner of creation lives to testify.

For as long as I shall live
I will testify to love
I'll be a witness in the silences when words
are not enough
With every breath I take I will give thanks
to God above
For as long as I shall live
I will testify to love.

From the mountains to the valleys
From the rivers to the sea

Every hand that reaches out
Every hand that reaches out to offer peace
Every simple act of mercy
Every step to kingdom come
All the hope in every heart will speak what
love has done.

About the Writers

SHAE COOKE is grateful that even divorce could not separate her from the love of Jesus Christ. She writes from beautiful Anmore, British Columbia, where her family and the magnificent natural wonders of her creative Father encourage her inspirational voice, revealed in print worldwide. Additionally, Shae jumps into the shoes of others as a ghostwriter. A former foster child, a mother, and now in a beautiful relationship, the Lord holds copyright to her testimony, which is a work in progress. Write her at P.O. Box 78006, Port Coquitlam, B.C. Canada V3B 7H5 or visit www.shaecooke.com.

TAMMY FITZGERALD graduated from Cedarville University with a degree in English Literature, and went on to become an editor at Destiny Image Publishers. She also recently completed her teacher's certification at Shippensburg University. She currently lives in Pennsylvania with her cat, and has her eyes open to see where in the world God will lead her next. Contact her at tcfitzgerald1984@hotmail.com.

DONNA SCUDERI is a former high school English teacher and one-time rock musician who has been writing and editing professionally for more than a decade. Having served nine years in the editing department of an international ministry, she now serves a variety of individuals and organizations to perfect their message through print and public speaking. She also recently completed a feature-length screenplay. Contact Donna at readywriter77@yahoo.com.

ANGELA RICKABAUGH SHEARS has been writing and editing for more than 20 years, although these trips to The Powder Room are her first out-from-behind-the-scenes books. She earned her B.A. from the University of Hawaii Manoa with a major in journalism/communications and a minor in political science. Angela, her husband Darrell, and their Old English Sheepdog Maggie, live in southcentral Pennsylvania... except when they are daydreaming about living back in Hawaii. Visit her Web site at www.writewordsnow.com.

RECOMMENDED READING

A Call to the Secret Place by Michal Ann Goll

Hope Beyond Reason by Dave Hess

How to Hear God's Voice by Mark and Patti Virkler

Living in His Presence by Richard Booker

The Happy Intercessor by Beni Johnson

The God Chasers by Tommy Tenney

The Prayer God Loves to Answer by Don Nori Sr.

The Significance of One by Steve Vanzant

What's Your Spiritual Quotient? by Mark Brewer

Additional copies of this book and other
book titles from DESTINY IMAGE are
available at your local bookstore.

Call toll-free: 1-800-722-6774.

Send a request for a catalog to:

Destiny Image® Publishers, Inc.

P.O. Box 310
Shippensburg, PA 17257-0310

*"Speaking to the Purposes of God for This
Generation and for the Generations to Come."*

**For a complete list of our titles,
visit us at www.destinyimage.com.**